PhilanthropyRoundtable

The Fabric of Character

A Wise Giver's Guide to Supporting Social and Moral Renewal

By Anne Snyder

Copyright © 2019, The Philanthropy Roundtable. All rights reserved.

Published by The Philanthropy Roundtable, 1120 20th Street NW, Suite 550 South, Washington, D.C. 20036

Free copies of this book are available to qualified donors. To learn more, or to order more copies, call (202) 822-8333, e-mail main@PhilanthropyRoundtable.org, or visit PhilanthropyRoundtable.org. A printed version is available from Amazon. A PDF may be downloaded at no charge at PhilanthropyRoundtable.org.

Cover: Ocskay Bence / Adobe Stock

ISBN 978-0-9978526-2-2
LCCN 2019933769

First printing, March 2019

Current Wise Giver's Guides from The Philanthropy Roundtable

The Fabric of Character:
A Wise Giver's Guide to Supporting Social and Moral Renewal
By Anne Snyder

Uniform Champions:
A Wise Giver's Guide to Excellent Assistance for Veterans
By Thomas Meyer

Learning to Be Useful:
A Wise Giver's Guide to Supporting Career and Technical Education
By David Bass

Catholic School Renaissance:
A Wise Giver's Guide to Strengthening a National Asset
By Andy Smarick and Kelly Robson

Clearing Obstacles to Work:
A Wise Giver's Guide to Fostering Self-Reliance
By David Bass

Agenda Setting: A Wise Giver's Guide to Influencing Public Policy
By John J. Miller and Karl Zinsmeister with Ashley May

Excellent Educators:
A Wise Giver's Guide to Cultivating Great Teachers and Principals
By Laura Vanderkam

From Promising to Proven:
A Wise Giver's Guide to Expanding on the Success of Charter Schools
By Karl Zinsmeister

Closing America's High-achievement Gap: A Wise Giver's Guide to Helping Our Most Talented Students Reach Their Full Potential
By Andy Smarick

Blended Learning: A Wise Giver's Guide to Supporting Tech-assisted Teaching
By Laura Vanderkam

Serving Those Who Served:
A Wise Giver's Guide to Assisting Veterans and Military Families
By Thomas Meyer

Protecting Donor Intent:
How to Define and Safeguard Your Philanthropic Principles
By Jeffrey Cain

Transparency in Philanthropy
By John Tyler

For all current and future titles, visit PhilanthropyRoundtable.org/guidebook

TABLE OF CONTENTS

PREFACE

Character formation is one of the most vital and most overlooked needs in America today. It cuts across all walks of life, means somewhat different things to different people, and is not readily susceptible to the metrics by which we often define success. It is hard, vulnerable, interpersonal work. It is missing from many corners of modern life.

In 2016 The Philanthropy Roundtable stepped into this space with a new initiative led by Anne Snyder. Through intensive workshops, consultations, site visits, and a retreat, Anne has assembled a national network of inspired practitioners and a small but dedicated group of donors who have made character formation central to their vision.

Three years on, we are pleased to publish this new guidebook—which profiles some of the most exemplary organizations engaged in the difficult process of reviving the country's moral consciousness, one small community at a time. Six of these are examined in great depth, with other noteworthy examples included, and the overarching principles that unite them explained in a usable toolkit.

As the stories in this volume show, it's never too early or too late to invest in character formation. Some of the programs, like grade schools and youth clubs, work on instilling humane values when children are most receptive—a sadly lacking component of much education today. Others, like a rehab and workforce re-entry program, do the essential work of walking with ex-offenders and addicts on the long road back from their darkest point, putting grit and gristle into the American ideal of second chances. Then there are those that encompass multi-generational communities—such as a neighborhood revival now gone international—which illustrate how successful character-building is not just an individual but a truly communal effort.

As different as these programs are in their aims and methods, they all share certain elements in common. To draw those out, and consider how your own organization can model and encourage healthier behavior, turn to the 16 Questions: a potentially transformative tool for groups of all stripes—nonprofit, corporate, public service, and beyond. We invite you to join us in this character revival.

We are grateful to the Kern Family Foundation and the John Templeton Foundation for their invaluable support to launch and sustain this unique initiative.

The Philanthropy Roundtable exists to help American donors pursue their charitable goals as effectively as possible. If there is some way we can assist you in refining your giving, elevating fellow citizens, and strengthening our free society, please let us know.

And let us know at Main@PhilanthropyRoundtable.org or 202.822.8333 if you have colleagues you would like to receive copies of this book. (Print versions are also available at Amazon.)

Adam Meyerson
President
The Philanthropy Roundtable

Ulysses
A poem by Alfred, Lord Tennyson

An Excerpt

...The lights begin to twinkle from the rocks:
The long day wanes: the slow moon climbs: the deep
Moans round with many voices. Come, my friends,
'Tis not too late to seek a newer world.
Push off, and sitting well in order smite
The sounding furrows; for my purpose holds
To sail beyond the sunset, and the baths
Of all the western stars, until I die.
It may be that the gulfs will wash us down:
It may be we shall touch the Happy Isles,
And see the great Achilles, whom we knew.
Tho' much is taken, much abides; and tho'
We are not now that strength which in old days
Moved earth and heaven, that which we are, we are;
One equal temper of heroic hearts,
Made weak by time and fate, but strong in will
To strive, to seek, to find, and not to yield.

Character: A Definition

Character is a set of dispositions to be and do good, engraved on a person in multiple ways: by strong family attachments that teach what to love and how to love well; by regular habits that ingrain small acts of self-control; by teachers and role models who personify excellence and inspire emulation; by religious instruction on honest, courageous, and compassionate living; through institutions that establish standards for good conduct, and mentors who inculcate concrete ways to execute it; by the reading of great literature; through experiences of struggle, positions of responsibility, and the blessings and demands of enduring commitments. The habits of character grow best in contexts that are nurturing, orderly and predictable, with clear yet grace-infused feedback mechanisms, and an inspiring ideal in view.

Character is shaped on multiple levels, but the person of character has integrated those levels into a whole personality. The person of character can be counted upon to be reliable and predictable over time. He or she is stable in the face of moral temptation, and chooses right even when it is painful. A person of character responds authentically to value; her loves are ordered. To have character is to refuse anything that satisfies one's lower loves. It is to put aside our natural tendency toward pride and selfishness, and to seek instead the good of others, of a community, of country.

A Person of Character...

...is in love with the good.

...is graced by humility.

...is honest.

...keeps his or her word.

...is conscientious and diligent.

...is courageous in choosing to do the right thing, even when it's painful.

...is disciplined and self-controlled.

...is able to see the good in other human beings and draw it out.

...is generous and hospitable.

...perseveres when the going gets rough; possesses mental toughness.

...has such a honed moral instinct so as to be fully integrated— head, heart, and helping hand.

...refuses to choose a course of action based on popular opinion, but rather on a deeper sense of right versus wrong.

...takes responsibility for his or her mistakes.

...is a lifelong learner, never satisfied with his or her own shortcomings; continuously seeks wisdom.

...is self-possessed, and bestows dignity to all around him or her.

...puts others' well-being above his or her own.

...honors his or her commitments.

...is compassionate and empathetic.

...is grateful and gracious.

...forgives and seeks forgiveness.

...should be able to discern the quality of character in others.

INTRODUCTION

Why Character? Why Now?

When I hear the word "character," I confess I don't immediately jump up and down. There's a joyless starchiness to the word, the image of a strained schoolmarm about to wrap your knuckles. It carries historical baggage. There are so many different value systems now; isn't the time for a one-size-fits-all character revival over? Most pointedly for our purposes, of all the problems this country faces, is character really something that *philanthropists* should address?

And yet, there is interest. And not just interest, but some deep, uncommonly wide agreement that while life in the twenty-first century calls for character more than ever, the conditions under which good character is forged are in trouble—weakened as much by the decline of traditional institutions as by a culture that promotes "I" before "we," pleasure before purpose, self-expression before submission to a source of moral wisdom beyond oneself.

Simply put, there are no longer authoritative institutions that are widely trusted. Many of our countrymen disagree about the fundamental nature of the good, about what it means to be an American, about the requirements and rewards of citizenship. In one decade technology has re-wired our relationships to work, knowledge, place, and one another. There is a creeping sensation of split-level living between the real and the virtual, of compartmentalized identities and behaviors in a dozen different silos, all leading to widespread experiences of alienation and meaninglessness.

Some facts: Seven million prime-working-age men sit at home, idle and unemployed. Neighborliness is an increasingly rare experience, with only 31 percent of Americans socializing weekly with someone next door (down from 44 percent in 1974). More people live alone, eat alone, and displace real-time conversation with controlled (if frenetic) screen communion than ever before. Moral language has declined in both use and understanding, while a 2017 Gallup poll found that Americans' views of the state of our moral values as a society are themselves at a nadir (both conservatives and liberals were surveyed). Tribalism has replaced free and civil debate on college campuses. Two thirds of high-school students admit to cheating. More and more kids fail to perform simple developmental tasks, and there's widespread concern that young people lack the grit to see them through when the going gets tough.

There are also attitudinal shifts that perplex older generations familiar with a more traditional life script. Traditional markers of adulthood have eroded. People are getting married later, having kids later (if bearing children at all), hopping from job to job, and just generally following a scatterplot of ever-shifting commitments. The young express a crisis of purpose and moral direction, with higher rates of anxiety and even suicide. Religious observance is at record lows, along with rates of volunteerism and engagement in community organizations. Trust in public institutions continues to weaken, diminished further by the coarseness and dishonest public discourse perpetuated by our national leaders. "Fragmentation," "consumerism," "isolation," and "polarization" are perceived as symptoms *and* causes of our deeper malaise, and those who traditionally saw themselves as core to the great American middle now feel forgotten, excluded, and unneeded.

In all of this, alarmed citizens from a wide range of cultural backgrounds and political persuasions are looking to "character" as a kind of thread which, if sewn with care and intention, might stand a chance of restitching our fraying social fabric, or at least help mend its most jagged tears. There isn't full agreement as to the precise definition, but concern for it spans sectors, subcultures, and ideological factions.

And so people are rising up to respond. Across multiple domains, from education, to the marketplace, to a millennial generation's longings and demands, there's a kind of humanistic renaissance going on, a renaissance in which the needs of the whole person are getting a fresh hearing. You might call it the whole person revolution.

You see this in the classroom, where there is growing interest in providing a more holistic, personalized pedagogical palette, including project-based and social-emotional learning. You see this in medicine, with more patients wanting an integrated approach to health. You see it in the rise of shared workspaces and employers promising perks that suggest a concern for one's well-being and sense of purpose in the job. You even see it in efforts aimed at improving life in low-income neighborhoods, with increasing awareness that healthy relationships are key to any economic progress. There's simply a growing appreciation for human beings as more than utilitarian consumers, and this rediscovery invites "character"—and moral conversation generally—to pull up a chair and stay a while.

We see psychologists like Angela Lee Duckworth making real inroads with her research on grit, perseverance, and self-control at The Character Lab, gaining a wide hearing and finding application at places like KIPP Academies, West Point, even the Seattle Seahawks. The *New York Times* reported in January 2018 that Yale University's most popular class ever is called "Psychology and the Good Life," with 1,200 students enrolled to inquire into the sources of meaning and contentment. Books like David Brooks's *The Road to Character* and Brené Brown's work on courage and vulnerability have made a surprisingly big splash, revealing widespread interest in a revival of moral categories and vocabulary. An increasing number of philanthropic foundations are adding "character" and its synonyms to their giving portfolios.

What's missing is an organizing core. "Character" is alive and kicking, but right now it's a hodge-podge filled with well-intentioned factions, conferences, and research commissions. There is no unifying creed, and, perhaps more importantly, no concrete framework for action.

That is what this book is for. It is to provide philanthropists a fresh lens that they can use to evaluate initiatives that attempt to form character and transform lives. It offers examples of organizations that have succeeded at this task, and draws out some of their common characteristics. It hopes to inspire donors, practitioners, and our nation's leaders to see our current cultural moment as one that hungers for a revived moral consciousness, if only we could strengthen the conditions to awaken it.

My approach

This book begins as a modern-day inquiry into an age-old question: "How do people become who they are?" Put normatively, what are the pathways to forming the will, the mind, and the heart and soul of an individual such that he or she will be equipped to navigate life's vicissitudes with equipoise, courage, hope, and a loving knowledge of the good? What makes a great citizen, a faithful wife, an attentive father, an obedient yet curious child, a devoted teacher, a tireless and kind custodial staffer, a persevering student, a resilient soldier, a wise CEO, a prudent president?

When you put this task to people—"describe the development of your own character"—you usually get a three-part response. First, they usually cite the presence of a loving authority figure at an impressionable time of their lives. This could be a parent, a grandparent, a teacher, a coach. Second, they tend to recall some difficult struggle that forever after defined them, both in the scars it left and the strength it built. Third, they refer to a time when they became inspired to serve a cause greater than themselves, and served that cause with commitment and passion. In all three of these, there's repetition—if through different forms, with different faces—over a lifetime.

It's a pattern, some might even say a formula. But what's *not* formulaic is the most important caveat: these three elements have to be organic. You cannot manufacture love or struggle or even commitment and get authentic character. The three-part pattern does not translate into a machine where you put in raw materials and push out a perfect product. Life—the stuff of mystery and surprise, stakes and emotion—is *always* molding our character. It's never quite a done deal.

This is where philanthropy has often faltered. Especially today, using currencies of dollars and limited time horizons and theories of change and so much data, donors are naturally tempted to crave control of the outcomes, including the time it takes to achieve them. Donors try to confront character head-on, supporting programs that claim to impart it in one fell swoop, conducting research that dissects the complexity of human motivation into slices that can be measured and isolated for targeted interventions. An effort to teach empathy here, some grit training over there. While well-intended, such approaches too often treat the individual as if he or she lives in a static environment, making little difference in the communities and culture we need to see edified.

It doesn't have to be this way. There is an opportunity right now for the philanthropic imagination around character to be recast, away from a didactic focus on individuals towards a more *institutional* vision, one that's equipped to shape the moral ecologies that nurture growth. The question of the hour is: What characterizes those institutions that not only form us to be individuals of character, but also mold us into the sort of people who are faithful spouses, responsible parents, generous neighbors, self-governing citizens, resolute in a crisis and gracious at a picnic?

This book offers an initial sketch by inviting you in to the life and times of those institutions currently doing something special. Many scholars are working on a theory of character-building, and we want to encourage their efforts and build on their progress. But there are hundreds if not thousands of organizations that are already doing it. When it comes to character, the practice is often ahead of the theory. Our task is to learn from what exists, and to understand why it's succeeding.

To that end, I am going to suggest a list of 16 features that distinguish the most successful character initiatives across class and culture, life stage, and even service sector. I have investigated hundreds of these organizations, and noticed that the ones that work have certain traits in common. There are certain *conditions* present in them that run against today's rhythms and values. These conditions are communal in nature. They transcend walks of life. They are found in successful organizations in every social sector. They meet fundamental human needs.

The questions on the following page offer a framework for donors as they determine whether or not a potential grantee is fostering a community of character. These questions should be useful to philanthropists who want to evaluate their own organizations. They should aid those who want to create *new* institutions. And they can guide all those interested in restoring the broader middle ring of social capital that has been weakened, through a knowledge of what makes for a trustworthy institution that fosters healthy relationships and whole people.

One last note: Obviously, there are different ways to define what character is and how we as a society might better nurture its development. But most of the definitions fall into two categories. There is the individualistic view, which tends to be concerned with behaviors like honoring one's word, comporting oneself with civility and evenhandedness, persevering when the going gets rough, thinking about the long-term consequences of one's actions. And then there's more of a communitarian view, one that understands character in terms of a broad set of spiritual and moral longings that can only be satisfied through a web of vibrant communities that foster loving relationships, inspiring ideals, a system of accountability, and some greater purpose. To put it simply, the first view honors the power of human agency, the second the power of structural conditions.

My conviction is that somewhere between these two views is the truest vision. Somewhere between our need for traditional character-builders and our longing for innovative community-makers is where this inquiry needs to begin, and actually where American renewal has always begun. To address one without the other is like pouring new wine into old wineskins, futile and a waste. Good character and vibrant community are interdependent, and so should their re-imagining be.

So join me in exploring these questions. I hope they advance the conversation around character and community in ways that unify what is currently a loose network of donors, doers, and thinkers. And I hope it inspires you to look at your own life and sphere of influence with fresh eyes to the institutional landscape undergirding both, a landscape in dire need of moral replenishment and the human touch.

16 QUESTIONS:
An Organizational Guide
for Great Character Formation

"By their fruit you shall know them…"

The world is full of organizations that seek to transform character and improve lives, but how can you tell which ones are successful and which ones aren't?

The following questions should provide a guide to help you make these judgment calls. They fall into 16 categories, corresponding to the 16 crucial features that truly formative institutions tend to possess:

1. **TELOS:** Does the organization have a clear, strong reason for being in the world, embraced and pursued by all of its members? Does it give its members organizing criteria for what to love?

2. **LITURGIES & RITUALS:** Is there a covenant or creed that is affirmed regularly as a community, in word and deed? Are there communal rhythms, routines, and rituals?

3. **FULL ENGAGEMENT by ALL MEMBERS:** Are all members of the organization, regardless of position or stature, engaged in the mission and aware of the significance and contribution of their roles?

4. **POWER of the PARTICULAR:** Does the organization have a particular identity, a thick set of norms that gets passed on to its members? Does it have a unique quality that is recognizable in those it has shaped?

5. **WHOLE PERSON:** Does the organization have a clear conception of the whole person—head, heart, and helping hand—and seek to develop it? Are employees and departments integrated across domains, serving constituents in complementary, mutually reinforcing ways?

6. HEALTHY RELATIONSHIPS: Does the institution put relational health as the foundation for its success? Does the organization foster social trust? Does it have a strong sense of community?

7. TECH-WISE: Is the institution careful about the latest technological advance, embracing it insofar as it promotes healthy relationships and individual skill, and setting limits when it makes those objectives more difficult?

8. INTENTIONAL PLURALISM: Does the institution foster opportunities to relate to those unlike yourself? Are members consistently exposed to other worlds, trained in the arts of civility, deep listening, and cross-cultural agility?

9. STRUGGLE & GROWTH: Are there opportunities for growth and tests of character? Does the organization have a process by which such struggles are given meaning and direction?

10. VULNERABILITY & ACCOUNTABILITY: Has psychological safety been established such that individuals feel free to be honest? Is there a structure of mutual accountability?

11. REFLECTION: Are there built-in processes for reflection, and excavation of one's inner life and public fruits?

12. EXEMPLARS: Are there attentive and conscientious authority figures who serve as role models, coaches, and mentors? Does the leader set the character standard for the organization?

13. AGENCY & INITIATIVE: Are members of the organization empowered to act, create, initiate? Are they encouraged to be responsible moral agents, not simply passive consumers?

14. JOY: Is there joy in the house? Are hospitality and unconditional welcome a key part of the institution's DNA?

15. TRANSFORMATION: Are there consistent testimonies of whole-person change in a positive direction?

16. GENERATIVITY: When people depart from this formative institution, do they promote a similar culture in other contexts? Has the institution imparted a set of ideals that members want to live up to ever after?

It's important to note that the features of effective character-building institutions are fundamentally interrelated: they are both interdependent and mutually reinforcing. This is particularly key in today's philanthropic and academic climates, which tend to cobble together a creed out of lots of disparate pieces. Instead, we should understand the fabric of character as precisely that: a fabric—interwoven, and much of the time, indivisible.

Feel free to test these against your own experience. When you reflect upon the most profound encounters in your own life, the most transformative institutions and relationships, do the memories share the above characteristics? You may be attracted to some traits over others, depending on your area of interest, expertise, and foundation portfolio. That is fine. Start with what resonates. In the pages ahead I will peel apart the questions and the contexts that best embody them. Oftentimes these organizations struggle to articulate the magic that makes them work; a common weakness that could almost be included in this list of signaling criteria. They instead succeed at the most demanding of tasks: transforming souls, and cultivating character by way of a healthy ecology of norms and relationships.

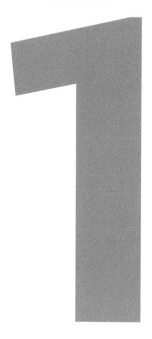

"For the Children's Sake"
The Oaks Academy
Indianapolis, Indiana

The question is not,—how much does the youth know? when he has finished his education—but how much does he care? And about how many orders of things does he care? In fact, how large is the room in which he finds his feet set? And, therefore, how full is the life he has before him?...

The child brings with him into the world not character but disposition. He has tendencies which may need only to be strengthened, or, again, to be diverted or even repressed. His character—the efflorescence of the man wherein the fruit of his life is a-preparing—is original disposition, modified, directed, expanded by education; by circumstances; later, by self-control and self-culture; above all, by the supreme agency of the Holy Ghost, even where that agency is little suspected, and as little solicited.

*~ **Charlotte Mason, British education reformer, 1923***

Margee Boswell was at her wits' end. Devon, a first grader, was acting out and blaming everyone but himself for his aggressive behavior. Not only were his teachers feeling increasingly helpless, but his patterns were wrecking the learning environment for the other students.

Boswell, the director of early-childhood education at The Oaks Academy, had one last thing to try. Coaxing the squirming boy into her office, she said, "Devon, I'm wondering if your conscience has gotten really, really small."

He stared at her, bewildered.

"My what?" Devon asked.

"Your conscience," Boswell said, as if it was his forearm, or his sweater, or some prized possession.

"What's that?" Devon asked.

She explained it to him. She said the conscience is like a muscle that signals the appropriate course of action. She said each one of us has one, regardless of whether we're aware of it, listen to it, or exercise it. Devon took it in, unusually quiet. He didn't like that a fundamental part of him was somehow undersized.

"Now, your conscience appears to have shrunken," Boswell said, "but I think there's a way we might be able to grow it back to normal size."

Devon's eyes grew big. "How do we do that?" he asked.

"Well," Boswell explained, "when you've done something, and you really know you did it, you just say to the person you offended, 'Yes, I did that. Will you forgive me?' And as you continue to do that, over and over, I think your conscience will start growing again." She paused, her eyes sparkling. "It might even get back to normal size."

Devon was sold. He returned to the classroom, and from that day on, began admitting to his teachers when he made a mistake and apologizing to his peers when he let his temper get the better of him.

Welcome to The Oaks Academy, a network of independent schools founded in 1998 that believes deeply in the power of learning to find and use one's moral muscles. Blending a classical educational approach with the philosophy of early-twentieth-century British educator Charlotte Mason, The Oaks has developed a learning model that is serving the most racially and socioeconomically diverse student body in urban Indianapolis. The students at its two elementary campuses and one middle school are 50 percent low-income, 25 percent middle-income, and 25 percent higher-income. They are 40 percent black, 40 percent white, and 20 percent biracial, Asian, or Hispanic.

And these schools top the charts not only on test scores, but on community strength and cohesion, too. The Oaks grounds itself in four core values: (1) Study and celebrate truth, goodness, and beauty; (2) Recognize the personhood of each child; (3) Act as a catalyst for renewal; (4) Ensure that relationships come first in all interactions. Such are the conditions for what The Oaks does with distinction, that of forming the will and ordering desires, choice after choice, habit after habit.

The child is a person

Charlotte Mason grounded her theory of education in four key pillars: (1) The Child Is a Person, (2) Education Is a Discipline, (3) Education Is a Science of Relations, and (4) Education Is a Life. They are interdependent to a great extent, yet to understand them concretely, and in contemporary context, I am going to take each as an individual axiom and see how together they inform the norms that govern The Oaks's educational approach.

"Our motto borrows from St. Augustine," says Boswell. "I am, I can, I ought, I will." In other words:

1. *I am*—We have the power of knowing ourselves.
2. *I can*—We are conscious of power to do what we perceive we ought to do.
3. *I ought*—We have within us a moral judge to whom we feel ourselves subject, who points out and requires of us our duty.
4. *I will*—We determine to exercise that power with a volition that is in itself a step in the execution of what we will.

The Oaks begins from the place of dignifying the child—both the child's potential, and his or her agency. There is no applying education *to* children, but rather helping them see themselves as learners. The Oaks believes that children are not blank slates or "embryonic oysters" who have the potential of becoming persons; they are *born* persons, capable of rising to high standards of behavior and honoring proper authority. "The concepts of authority and obedience are true for all people whether they accept them or not," wrote Mason in her book, *A Philosophy of Education*. "Submission to authority is necessary for any society or group or family to run smoothly. Authority is not a license to abuse children, or to play upon their emotions or other desires, and adults are not free to limit a child's education or use fear, love, power of suggestion, or their own influence over a child to make a child learn."

Education is a discipline

If there's one thing The Oaks does with distinction, it's habit development. There is a lot of excitement these days around forming good habits—from Charles Duhigg, author of *The Power of Habit*, to popular panels at the South by Southwest festival, to a distracted and overwhelmed generation yearning for control and focus. But the deeper habits of will—of moral choosing, day in and day out—are often less discussed.

Beginning in third grade and continuing through eighth, Oaks students take time each semester to write about their habit development before reading the essay aloud in front of their classmates and parents.

"When the kids come to parent-teacher conferences, they're reflecting on their growth in these areas and leading that overall discussion," says Laura Grammer, The Oaks's award-winning middle-school principal. "It's not people putting this on them." There's also a level of vulnerability and understanding that "this is what we're doing together and here's where I am."

> Children are not blank slates who have the potential of becoming persons; they are born persons, capable of rising to high standards of behavior and honoring proper authority.

Work begins in the youngest grades to model and support the following habits: Attention, Obedience, Respect, Responsibility, Reflection, Reverence, Punctuality, Thoroughness, Integrity, Self-Control, and Service. Instead of a curricular component confined to a certain day or week of the year, these habits are embedded in all interactions. Teachers know their students well and support them in weak areas by providing repeated opportunities for practice, self-correction, and success. Teachers also provide natural consequences when needed, and avoid manipulating students with "carrot and stick" incentives, which tend to result in resentment, or only temporary behavior change.

In Charlotte Mason's writing on education as a discipline, she noticed that parents and teachers would sometimes dismiss a child's lack of responsibility or maturity as an innate character flaw, instead of seeing it as a weakness that could be improved. At The Oaks, the whole philosophy is rooted in the conviction that each person has the capacity to develop these habits.

"Every person has attention," says Boswell. "You must choose to give it. It's not our job to grab your attention, and keep your attention. It's *your* job, and *your* duty, to give your attention to the matter at hand." The students are the actors in control of themselves.

As you might expect, with screens everywhere kids now enter The Oaks with less self-regulation than before. "We love technology as a tool," says Boswell, "but we don't think it has any place in the classroom." At the young ages, The Oaks encourages make-believe play, so that whatever roles student assume, they must abide by certain rules. (This is especially powerful for kids who don't come from neighborhoods where it is safe to play.) The goal is to become familiar with what it is to rise up to the proper standard, to grow into a particular virtue.

"Children have two guides to help them in their moral and intellectual growth"—"the way of the will" and "the way of reason," wrote Mason. "Children must learn the difference between 'I want' and 'I will.' They must learn to distract their thoughts when tempted to do what they may want but know is not right, and think of something else, or do something else, interesting enough to occupy their mind. After a short diversion, their mind will be refreshed and able to will with renewed strength."

Education is the science of relations

An Oaks education is deeply humanistic, grounding both its pedagogical approach and disciplinary action in relationships. "The idea is that the more relationships you apprehend both with people and with knowledge," says Boswell, "the more serviceable you are."

By the time they get to eighth grade, Oaks students have to write three essays and reflect on them with their parents and a school administrator. The essays explore questions like: What has been my spiritual journey? What is truth? What is beauty? This helps them ponder: What *is* truth? Do I believe in truth? How do I identify truth? What *is* beauty? How can I be an agent to create beauty in the world? The hope is to marry the reflections on personal growth with all the art, beauty, music, and language that they've related to throughout their education.

"It's amazing to see our 13- and 14-year-olds wrestling with these deep ideas," says Grammer. The idea is that they develop a love for truth, beauty, and goodness, and that their affections are shaped by what they are steeped in.

The Oaks's approach to discipline works similarly. When new teachers tour The Oaks for the first time, they see a disarming joy of relationship going on in the classrooms, where teachers are not motivating by way of threatening words or exciting promises.

"Don't get me wrong," says Grammer, "Our kids mess up. They do all the same things that other kids do. They hit each other. They bully. But they come and sit in front of you, and you say, 'Okay, tell me what you did. What could you have done differently?' And you have a dialogue with the child where he is taking ownership over his relationships. 'How are you going to make this right? What relationship did you damage? Did you steal time from somebody? Did you steal a sense of safety? Did you steal honor and respect that was due to someone? Okay. How do you restore honor? How do you pay back time?' They start to see their behavior in a relational context. Not in a 'what are they getting out of it and how to make their life better' context. They're in rich relationships with *people*."

The hope is that a moral sense develops that ultimately sees bad behavior as something that tears if not breaks relationships. Students are encouraged to think less about self, and more about shalom.

"Horrible things are going to happen to them in their life," says Grammer. "They're going to have a parent get sick and die, or get divorced. Or they're going to be in an accident, or they're going to unintentionally hurt somebody. How do you go on from that? Well, it's the wealth of relationships that they create around them. And our students get a chance to reflect on this," to learn what an authentic relationship requires and gives.

Teachers at The Oaks are trained to discern the particular reason for misbehavior. Is it ignorance: they didn't understand the expectations? Is it weakness: they need support to do the right thing, as we all do at times? Or is it rebellion?

"The first thing you do is ask the child: 'What did you hear me say? Can you tell me what you're supposed to do?' We're asking them questions, never telling them what it is they did. If they really didn't understand, then we just inform. Ignorance needs to be informed. You give them support. 'Okay. We're going to practice this until you get it. You know how to walk down the stairs, you know you're not supposed to jump, we're just going to practice that! Show me you can do it.'"

But, Boswell continues, if "you've told them what to do, and broken it down into little steps so that anybody who wanted to do it could do it, and they won't, then we have to look at it as rebellion." This is where The Oaks's relational cornerstone comes in.

"If they've rebelled," says Boswell, "they've broken relationship. They've essentially taken themselves out from underneath good authority, so they're removed. Isolation is the primary consequence for rebellion. And isolation can work because when you're alone, your conscience finally has the ability to speak to you."

"At some point they'll tell you what they did," Boswell continues, "they'll confess it. And I'll say to them, 'How do you feel about that?' And so often, they'll just start weeping. They'll say, 'I feel bad.' And I'll say, 'Oh, that's good.' And they'll look at me like I'm crazy. 'Why is this *good?*' "

> By the time students graduate, they will have given 392 memorized recitations, some as short as a Bible verse, others as long as the Gettysburg addresss.

"This feeling tells you that you have a conscience," she'll respond. "When you do something bad, you're supposed to feel bad. I'd feel bad if I did that too. But you don't have to stay feeling bad. Let's work through it. There's a way to get the bad feelings out. And that is, you go back to the person, you tell them what you did, and you ask them to forgive you. Forgiveness is the only thing that cleanses that."

From pre-K on, The Oaks is training children in this pattern of contrition and forgiveness and restoring relationships. "We say here that relationships come first," says Boswell. "We will do whatever it takes to restore a relationship, because once that child's relationship is restored, then they're okay. They can go back in and they can learn. Otherwise, they've got all this emotional stuff going on, and they're not listening anyway. They're not willing to engage."

In the midst of discipline, The Oaks is careful not to shame the child. "We teach our teachers, never tell a child that you're disappointed in him or her. Disappointment expresses surprise and disgust and 'how could you?' Do we want our spouses or our friends to say, 'I'm so disappointed in you'? When someone told you they were disappointed in you, you remember that. So we just peel back those words and teach our teachers to ask the student, 'How are you feeling?' They know. They know from a very early age. If you want to develop their conscience, treat them like they have a conscience. Make sure that they can look inward and say, 'I knew that was wrong,' rather than telling them it was wrong. If they have a conscience, you've got to let them feel it."

Education is a life

"I think one of the most tragic things that's happening in American school systems today is how we manipulate children's motivations by way of external praise and punishment," says Grammer. "Do the right thing and you will always get rewarded" is not how real life works, so giving kids that illusion can be damaging. "If you're constantly in a school system where people are motivating you by prods and carrots and sticks, that's how you come to respond. But there are smart kids who figure out, 'Hey, it's worth it to just put up with consequences if I can actually take some control of my life.' So you come to find out in classrooms, it's always the same kids who are considered the bad kids. And always the same kids that are feeling really good about how they're doing with no hard change. Because they know how to play the game."

No Oaks classroom has a clip-up or clip-down status slide, marble goals, or candy rewards. "Why is getting an A on a test worth a piece of candy?" Grammer asks. "That knowledge you learned is so valuable. It just cheapens it" to equate it to a chunk of sugar.

Knowledge is rather like a treasure to discover and nurture. Oaks students memorize unusual quantities of poetry, sacred texts, and historic speeches. By the time they graduate they'll have done 392 different recitations. Some of these are as brief as a Bible verse while others are as long as the Gettysburg Address.

"To cheapen [those recitations] to a sticker," says Grammer, "when those words that they have graven on their hearts and minds, of great ideas…we are numbing a whole generation of kids by equating candy, pizza, stickers and certificates to knowledge."

The Oaks is also of the mind that such feedback loops give kids a false sense of who they are in relationship to each other and the world— both the "good" kids and the "bad" kids. "The moment you get critiqued, you crumble. As soon as you realize you did something wrong, you ask, 'What's wrong with me and my value?'"

When you visit elite college campuses today, it's striking how out-wardly driven students are, how sensitive to external feedback. Millennials are simultaneously stressed and coddled. Often their sense of self seems driven by acclaim of others, which can lead to poor decision-making, unnecessary anxiety, and a hyper-sensitivity to uncomfortable content.

The Oaks offers preventative medicine, training young people to make decisions based on internalized standards of the good. When an award is given to an Oaks student, it's a private thanks granted by the teacher. Commendation of a job well done, yes, but there's no fanfare, no ego oxygen that might grant a false sense of identity that will only slow them down later in life.

"We want to teach them to be a good friend, or a spouse, or a dependable employee, or a doctor driven by good ethics, when you don't always get noticed for doing the right thing," says Grammer. "We want children who are motivated internally to continue to choose to do the right thing even when there is no tangible or immediate reward for that."

Training the teachers *away from* behavioral-management techniques is almost as tough as trying to counteract the logic perpetuated in many households.

"Teachers and parents [deal in conditional love] without even realizing the deeper implications, because it works on the surface level," says Grammer. "Children *want* to get rewarded. We crave to be recognized and appreciated; it feeds right into our pride and our fear and our guilt."

The problem is, parents and teachers "don't see how they are creating praise junkies by over-praising rather than encouraging. There are all these studies now about 'our kids need grit,' 'they need perseverance.' And yet this is what you are doing? They don't see that what you are doing is taking those traits away from them, because the fact is their will is something that has to be exercised. Just like you have to practice over and over again to get good at shooting a basketball, or reading, or math facts. If you are not given the opportunity to choose to do the right thing yourself, you cannot strengthen your own will."

The Oaks spends serious time training its incoming teachers to unlearn many of their starting assumptions. "Our professional development for them starts from the moment they sit down with us at the interview table," says Boswell. There's a week of new faculty orientation, mentors and observations in classrooms, and workshops with parents throughout the year.

"A lot of it is about changing the language for those" with moral authority, says Grammer. "Because so much of this is about people wanting a program that they can buy and put in their school. So teachers and school administrators can say, 'This is our character development program. This is how we intrinsically motivate our kids.' But the fact is, character is never something you can put on the kids; it's how you live life with them." This living alongside "is shaped entirely by what the teachers believe about children and people. If they don't believe our fundamental conviction that children are persons, then [character development] can't work in a classroom."

When an award is given to a student, it is a private thanks, rather than a fanfare. The goal is children who choose to do the right thing even when there is no immediate reward.

A generative seedbed—*E Pluribus Unum*

When it comes to character crucibles, there are few more pronounced than those awkward tween years from sixth to eighth grade. Hormones are flowing. The kids are more socially aware and insecure. When I met with Grammer in her principal's office, she had just ushered out a couple of crying 13-year-olds. "Middle schoolers act like little adults, and then they act like pre-K students. One minute they're throwing a temper fit and the next minute you're thinking, 'Wow, that was amazing. I'm learning from you.'"

The key is to continue to treat them like people, Grammer says. "Too many adults get so emotionally enmeshed with kids, rather than allowing them to struggle through whatever they're dealing with. Don't take it personally. We try to rescue them too often from the struggle, from these hard emotions."

Oaks kids are used to being around people from different backgrounds, but by the time middle school arrives, they start to wrestle with the implications of social difference. "We don't say we're colorblind around here," says Grammer. "But middle school is when they're really starting to develop their identity separate from their parents. They're trying to figure out where they stand in the world and with peers."

Some kids come from a rough street culture, for instance. When you get offended, you're expected to take revenge and fight back. When someone comes to us with this issue, we've learned never to say, "Don't fight back." That's just not okay to communicate to a young man who has grown up in a culture where honor and even survival demands that you fight for everything. Instead we say, "Listen, you stand up for what's right. Here are some words you can use: You tell them that it is never okay, and you say it strongly. Your impulse to fight back is good…. But how do you harness that in the best way?"

It's always a dialogue at The Oaks, to find the virtuous response while taking cultural contexts into account. "We believe every person at the core has the same needs and desires: to be seen and known for who they are, and loved in spite of everything."

The schools teach classical tales from around the world, showcasing non-Western musical traditions, presenting historical points of view and philosophies from both victors and the downtrodden. Everyone is taught how to dance, by eighth grade having learned at least eight historical dances from around the world.

In middle school, the students are assigned to a house, where identities form not around economic status or race but around universal virtues— *Veritas* (truth), *Animus* (bravery), *Fidelitas* (faithfulness), *Dignitas* (dignity). Students talk often about what their house name means and why it's important. The houses do regular service projects, and off-campus activities like camping trips provide built-in leadership opportunities for eighth-graders to mentor sixth-graders. Students gain a sense that they're part of something bigger than themselves, something foundational to all the other aspects of their identity.

"Teaching character requires returning to some basic principles of human flourishing, human relating, and lifelong learning," Oaks CEO Andrew Hart says. It's interesting: Given the school's diverse demographics and today's conventional wisdom, you'd expect more conversations to deal with issues of trauma and structural injustice. And those conversations happen, but The Oaks is proof that a cultural climate motivating kids to take hold of their own agency takes care of many of the other issues.

Mentoring and leadership opportunities abound, and a broader sense of school-as-family pervades the halls. The atmosphere is welcoming, from cozy armchairs in the hallway to classical music in a first-grade painting class. There's always one time a year that each grade level comes to the middle school—whether it's algebra students leading an activity on exponential growth with the first-graders, or the fourth-graders coming over and the seventh-graders taking them into the science lab for frog dissection. The eighth-graders go to the lower-school campuses to do service in the classrooms, with younger eyes watching.

Grammer credits former head of school and now CEO Andrew Hart with modeling the importance of relationality from the moment kids step out of the car. Every morning he and the other school leaders stand on the curb to greet every family and child by name as they arrive. Then everyone gathers for a song in the open hallway, parents often sticking around to center themselves before the work day begins.

"We have a parent community that's just so diverse, socioeconomically and racially, and so committed to our model…. The Oaks has become community for our parents," says Hart. Parents mix who would have never had the opportunity to cross paths. A kid from a wealthy neighborhood goes to a birthday party in an inner-city neighborhood. Suspicions ease and awkwardness melts as the shared backdrop of The Oaks takes center stage. "There's nothing like experience," says Boswell. "There's nothing like relationships."

Results, resources, and replication

The Oaks is changing the lives of teachers, families, and of course kids, but equally notable is the mark it's made on the larger city of Indianapolis. It serves as a point of light, of diversity as strength, of a cultivation of the model citizen and beloved neighbor. "Teachers come to The Oaks and say that their careers have been saved," says Boswell, who's hired and mentored dozens of Oaks teachers over the school's 20 years. Student alumni return often on their days off, wanting to say hello and relive fond memories.

There are 400 of these alumni so far, and high schools show keen interest in recruiting them. Some of the schools that cost as much as $20,000 a year will find financial aid for Oaks graduates because of their distinctive self-command, ability to relate to others, and engagement with ideas at a superior level. Most Oaks grads make honor rolls at their respective high schools, regardless of background. And teachers at these high schools say that the students who come to them from The Oaks are consistently "mature," "leaders," and "comfortable in their own skin."

In the beginning The Oaks's revenue consisted of an even split of tuition and philanthropy. That was the model for a dozen years. Then in 2010, the state of Indiana launched a program that allowed individuals or businesses to be eligible for up to a 50 percent tax credit if they donated money to a nonprofit that helps low- or moderate-income families pay for children using private schools. The Oaks chose to stay out of the voucher program in its first year, to be sure there were no encumbering strings attached. But once it became clear that there would be minimal interference from the state with curriculum, hiring, or other key elements of school operation, The Oaks opted in.

Today, The Oaks still covers about 35 percent of its budget through private donations raised from 500-600 donors per year. In 2017-18, that was $3.4 million. The Oaks received funding from the Walton Family Foundation, the Drexel Fund, and some other national entities to scale up its campuses. Increasingly, though, it relies on local philanthropists, plus the donated funds that are channeled through the state program.

At present, about 19 percent of Oaks families pay full tuition. Everyone else is on some form of scholarship, but almost all pay something to make sure students and families have skin in the game.

This model of affordable, high-quality, boundary-crossing education built on a moral core has sparked interest in other parts of the country. The Field School, which opened its doors on the south side of Chicago in 2018, was inspired by The Oaks blend of character training, classical education, and Charlotte Mason philosophy. A group of parents in Charlotte, North Carolina, are organizing to establish an offshoot in their city. A hedge-fund executive in San Francisco has offered to provide funding to start Oaks Academies in all the voucher states around the country.

Andrew Hart and his colleagues are studying their options. Should they expand further in their home city and state? Spend energy and resources to jump to new regions? Help allies plant similar schools elsewhere on their own?

"It's been our dream all along to proliferate this model," says Hart. Trying to package their success into transferable formulas, however, would be tricky. The secrets to the success of the academies—intimate relationships, very selective hiring, family involvement, and so forth—are resistant to shortcuts.

"Right now, we just don't know," admits Hart. "We're exploring writing an open-source cookbook describing what it takes to start the kind of culture we have, and sustain the model." Maybe, he wonders aloud, "we should just have people come and visit and be inspired. Do we embrace and feed more ed tourism? Or do we actively pursue educational entrepreneurs who want to incubate our model?" Everything from curriculum, teacher development, by-laws, and policy handbooks, to guidance on governance, mission statements, and fundraising strategies would have to be spelled out. Already, The Oaks is sharing some of its discoveries through something called the Indiana School Leader Fellowship, a network that connects principals across the state.

A kind of city-on-a-hill model, inspiring proliferations that are appropriate to their local contexts, currently seems most practical. The essential starting point for any replication in another city, Hart notes, is having outstanding leaders. "You have to find the right creator, as well as founding families, and trustees that are in it for the long haul."

Meanwhile, The Oaks is still refining its own practices. "We hope to expand the implementation of character and virtue development, as well as devise a meaningful system of evaluation, especially since we view character as an integrated part of the educational philosophy instead of a stand-alone curricular element. The Oaks has been asked by other schools and organizations across the country to share information about the implementation and benefits of habit formation."

For now, that generous leadership seems to be The Oaks's greatest contribution to a world eager for its magic. As a Proverb says: "Above all else, guard your heart, for everything you do flows from it."

Transformation
The Other Side Academy
Salt Lake City, Utah

The content of your character is your choice. Day by day, what you choose, what you think and what you do is who you become.
~ Heraclitus

Souls are like athletes that need opponents worthy of them, if they are to be tried and extended and pushed to the full use of their powers.
~ Thomas Merton

Freedom never is obtained by mere release from old limitations; freedom is the positive substitution of inward self-control for external restraints.
~ Harry Emerson Fosdick

Sometimes you find the most dazzling moral superstars in the unlikeliest of places.

My humbling moment came in walking through the back door of The Other Side Academy in Salt Lake City. I'd heard about it through an acquaintance who had discovered TOSA when his wife was surfing Yelp reviews, looking for a better moving company than the last disaster.

"Look, honey, these guys get five stars." She beckoned him over. "Would you believe this praise?"

Sure enough, every review for "The Other Side Movers" commended exceptional integrity, swiftness, punctuality, and care. Shortly after establishment, it shot to being the number-one rated moving company in Salt Lake City, and has remained there since. But reading a little closer, a curious tagline deepened the intrigue: "We rebuild lives by moving yours."

The Other Side Movers hail from The Other Side Academy, a life-training school for people with long criminal or addiction histories. Students commit to a minimum of a two-year residence—many as an alternative to incarceration—after prison sentences of five or more years (some have been in and out of jail for 20). Anyone who appears to be sincerely committed to changing his or her life is admitted free of cost, and the whole program is self-supporting.

"Our students might have some wild tattoos," reads a marketing brochure for The Other Side Movers, "but they are the hardest working, friendliest, most polite, and the most careful movers you can find. We take care of you as though our lives depended on it—because they do."

It begins with truth and love, every minute learned by doing. Entering this peer-to-peer residential community as "moral pea-brains," as founder Joseph Grenny puts it, within two or more years these former criminals catapult to "calculus-level" moral reasoning and relational maturity. It's not therapy, and it's not about relapse prevention. The Other Side Academy is about behaviors, and re-calibrating one's moral compass through practice and revelation.

"You'll solve your drug problem [here] and never even talk about it," says director Dave Durocher, who himself spent 25 years floating in and out of jails before landing at Delancey Street in California, one of the most effective rehab organizations in the country and the model inspiring The Other Side. "Once we have a value-centered life, we are not going to float away again."

TOSA only deals in real change. "This isn't a place where everybody gets what they deserve," says Grenny. "If you and I lived in a place where we all got what we deserved, nobody would ever get better. So the real question here is: What are we willing to *do*? What is the expression of who we are that we're willing to offer?"

What is it worth to save a life?

The Bench

It all starts with the Bench, an ordinary piece of furniture turned sacrosanct. Sitting in a crowded foyer in the back of the house, the Bench is like a portal from the old life to the new one—if you'll accept the truth and love it takes to change.

There are two ways to enroll at The Other Side Academy. You can either walk in off the street, or write a letter from jail. Most letters are desperate: "I'm at rock bottom." "I've realized I need change but I can't do it on my own." "Please help me. I promise I'm worth a shot."

> Brutal honesty is TOSA's hallmark. The purpose of the initial interview is to see if the applicant is willing to hear hard truth.

No one is ever turned down for an interview, but the admission process is rigorous. Only 10 percent of those who apply get in. Aside from non-negotiables like no arson, no sex offenders, and no psychiatric medication, the brutal honesty that is TOSA's hallmark turns many applicants away in the first encounter.

"Do you love your family?" a student I'll call Susan was asked during her first interview. She's now been at TOSA for a little over a year. "Of course I do," she remembers responding.

"No, you don't," came the reply, hard and swift. "You left them. You wouldn't be doing this crap to them if you loved them. I sure hate to see what you would do if you hated them."

Susan still sucks in her breath remembering the wake-up call. "That line right there was just…" she dwindles off. "I knew."

The purpose of that initial interview is to see if the person is willing to hear hard truth. There's a social contract established right from that first discussion. It says: "This is what your days are going to sound like for the next two years. Is this what you want to be hearing?"

"We really look for a fire in you," says a student I'll call Larry, who's been at TOSA for two years after serving multiple jail sentences. "There has to be something in there that we can mold and shape." Dave Durocher puts it simply: "What I'm looking for is a soul."

The Bench is at once a birthplace and a grave. "The idea is that [life] before the Bench doesn't exist anymore once you arrive," says Larry. "You have to put that behind you." At TOSA, past is prologue to the real living. Upon arrival, you get sent to the Bench for six hours, alone with your conscience, close to the door that could be your exit back to prison. A plaque on the wall for you to ponder outlines TOSA's 12 principles, your best hope for an alternate future (bold text as stated on the plaque; explanations adapted from the program literature):

• *You alone can do it, but you can't do it alone*
The bad choices we've made have disconnected us from our own best interests, and from other people. The way out is to let others in. We get to the Other Side by connecting to other imperfect people, because they are worth it. As they connect with us, we discover that we are worthy too.

• *Make and keep promises*
The only requirement for entry to The Other Side Academy is a sincere desire to change. We must learn a completely new set of habits and skills. Growth comes from making increasingly rigorous commitments to live by good principles.

• *Self-reliance, there is no free lunch*
We support ourselves by running businesses. If we don't work, we don't eat. The Other Side Academy is about us doing for ourselves what no one else can do for us.

• *Impeccable honesty*
In jails and rehab programs, we have perfected skills of lying, manipulating, and using those around us. Dishonesty has become such a habit that we are even disconnected from our own feelings and truths. These habits have kept us in a revolving door. To get to the *Other Side* you will be expected to practice impeccable honesty. You will be surrounded by others who hold you to account. This is the only path to having real relationships with others.

- *Act as if*

  New habits of self-discipline, hard work, and rigorous honesty will feel deeply uncomfortable—even painful—in the early stages. But as these new principles become new habits, they begin to create feelings of self-worth, peace, and happiness. Until then, we "act as if" we are honest, caring, curious, and humble. Over time we become that which we habitually do.

- *Embrace humility*

  Humility accelerates self-awareness. The speed with which we change is determined by the degree of our humility in listening to how others see us.

- *Each one teach one*

  Our past was about escaping discomfort and reacting to impulses. It was all about me. Stop thinking about yourself. As we lift and serve others we earn deep satisfaction. The Other Side Academy is a peer teaching system. Each time we learn a new skill, we are responsible for teaching it to others.

- *200% accountability*

  Everyone at The Other Side Academy is accountable not only for our own actions, but for watching over those around us. We need each other. Anyone who sees a problem is required to confront it and report it. The strength of our family is in everyone's commitment to keeping each other safe.

- *Forgiveness*

  Be patient with each other. We won't back down from letting you know when you fall short, but we won't give up on you. Grudges weaken our family and weigh down the one who carries them.

- *Boundaries*

  Maintaining boundaries is the process through which we create our character. The Other Side Academy has firm boundaries. The first ones are to avoid violence and avoid substance abuse. Set strong boundaries and be an example to others.

• *Faith-friendly*
There is no requirement at The Other Side Academy to believe in God or practice any particular religious beliefs. We are, however, supportive of beliefs that help you lead a healthier and more connected life. We worship and allow others to do the same.

• *Pride in work*
The best way to create a feeling of well-being is to do any job—no matter how minor—with joy and love. You get back what you put in. Measure the progress you are making by looking at the quality of your work. Shoddy work is an invitation to self-examination.

"We believe that changing from the outside in is a good place to start," says Durocher. The thesis is that when you practice living in the right way, for a long time, regardless of whether you feel like it or not, you begin to change. Add to that habitual right-choosing a supportive peer community who will hold you accountable, and a graduated tier of responsibility and autonomy, and little by little, crusty, angry, disillusioned skin starts to peel.

"People started to trust me," remembers Durocher of his own transformation. "That made me feel good. I started realizing, 'I can do this.' Then when some of those bigger responsibilities were given to me, and I was doing them well, I started to believe in myself."

With the inner change comes outer results. "I'm a hardworking, loyal person," he says. "Now I am honest," echoes Lola Zagey, a former heroin addict who helps run TOSA. Alan Fahringer, a third Delancey grad and current TOSA director, whose demon was methamphetamine, now calls himself "a person that has integrity. I take my word seriously. I'm a person that's *about* something."

What TOSA does, board chairman Grenny suggests, is help individuals rebalance their moral scales. "You can't undo the stuff that you did," he says. "You can't erase it. You've done so much damage, hurt so many people that your moral scales are never going to get fixed. All you can do is do more and more good and help and serve others until eventually you can feel inside yourself that shocking thought: 'Okay, maybe at this point I can be an okay person.'"

TOSA's entire model is peer-based: Everyone has either spent time in jail or struggled with drug addiction. This lends a foundational credibility—and, crucially, moral authority—because everyone has been through the same thing. There is no expert who swoops in, saying, "I'm going to fix you." Rather, it's "We're going to fix each other, and it doesn't matter how long it takes."

Games

"This is what we came for," Susan tells me, pointing to a drawer full of paper slips carrying raw scrawls in one of the busy passageways. "This is Games, how we change our behaviors."

It's a strange name for one of the most gut-punching rituals of TOSA life. But every student who blossoms into someone he or she can be proud of credits Games as the key. It's a twice-weekly circle where the wrongs of the week get broken down and addressed, to the offender's face. One student "pulls up" another by calling attention to some offense of house rules, then fills out a slip and puts it in the Games drawer. Come Tuesday or Friday, all the residents surround the offender with a tidal wave of feedback and exhortation. It gets colorful quickly.

"Oftentimes you're not even aware that you're doing something wrong. But we are telling you," says Susan. "We'll say, 'Hey Suzi, that's not appropriate.' And then other people will start jumping on that indictment, saying, 'Hey, come on, you're a leader. In this house, you know better. Come on, get it together.' It's a culture shock for every newcomer, especially those coming out of the prison ethos of 'no snitching.'"

"The last thing you ever do in jail is give feedback," says Susan. "But here, if I care about you, I will give you feedback." After many years, if not decades, of having families and the rest of society give up on you, the contrast of getting so much attention aimed at pulling you up to a higher moral standard—a standard that the community depends upon for its own functioning—is a radical change.

"We get visitors," says Grenny, and when the Games process is described to them, "they'll say, 'oh man, we've got to do something like that in my family.' And then you see a second thought come over their face, and they say, 'man, that would be terrifying. I would hate something like that.'"

He pauses here. "I think most of us in the normal world have this secret shame that causes us to cower from moral life. What TOSA does is force you" into moral judgments. "This moral life is available to the rest of us, but we don't choose to enter it. The question is, what are you aspiring towards? Do you want to enter a place of perfect truth? What if our students are teaching the rest of us that not only could we survive such a place, but it would actually elevate us as human beings. That a real, vulnerable accountability would make us all happier, more joyous and connected as people."

Goodbye to the past, goodbye to victimization

Contrary to conventional therapy practices, TOSA pushes students to avoid looking back. Whether the student's prior conception of self involves braggadocio or shame (it's typically a toxic mix of the two), TOSA believes it all needs to go. With the exception of some guided storytelling in the sophomore term, the past is off-limits.

"That image that you have of yourself…we're going to take that away from you," says Durocher. "We're not going to let you grow the mohawk, we're not going to let you grow the Fu Manchu mustache, we're not going to let you do all those things that you associated with prior. Instead, we're going to let you build a new image. But your new image is going to be built from you going forward, not who you thought you were when you got here."

> I used to believe that what happened to me in my childhood made me a victim. But I can make conscious choices and choose to do good instead of bad. It's up to me.

A student I'll call Joe served over 20 years in prisons from Nevada to Rhode Island, and is currently in his fifth month at TOSA. "Not talking about my past has been one of my biggest battles since I've been here," he admits. "I used to work all that past stuff with prison therapists. I'd just get in there and pull on their heartstrings, and force them in whatever direction I wanted. Here, that doesn't happen. We all drive each other in a positive direction."

He continues: "I used to believe that what happened to me in my childhood made me a victim. Which was why I acted in the ways I did. But all of us here, we're adults, and we can make conscious choices and choose to do good instead of bad. It's up to me. I have the choice to get up every morning and be happy and healthy, or I have a choice to get up and be depressed and angry."

Durocher chimes in: "A lot of people have horrific stories without making the bad decisions that we did. Going through life, you are going to get disappointed and people are going to hurt you. Get used to it. Learn to deal with bad circumstances and powerful emotions."

In the beginning, says Grenny, you have to "disconnect how you're feeling from how you're acting.... Numb yourself a little, so you don't act on impulse. Then figure out why you have these negative emotions. By the time you're a sophomore, you have a chance to sit with a group and start telling your story. But you need to learn to tell it in a new way, not in a glorifying, war story way, nor in a 'this is my identity' way, but in a way that takes some responsibility where you need to. And also absolves your responsibility for the things that weren't your choices. So often people feel either too much guilt or too little guilt."

At TOSA, all students both receive and give discipline and exhortation. Grenny and Durocher have discovered that accountability really only works when three or more are gathered. The freshman dorm has ten to a room. Later grades are four to eight per room. More broadly, informal critiquing and bolstering takes place all day long, as students work together, cook together, and clean together, scrutinizing and correcting each other as they go.

"I started set in my ways," says Joe. "I had this convict mentality, where I'd lived a certain way for so long that I thought my way was correct. So I was pretty thick-headed and stubborn when I got here. I didn't want to listen.... Somebody would try to correct me and I would immediately get angry. I'd curse them out: Who did they think they were?" Over time, Joe learned to trust the feedback, as he saw it came from people just like him, who had paid the price that allowed them to see things to which he was still blind.

"We're exactly the same," says Durocher about Joe. "The only difference is that I am farther removed. Everything that he's going through, I've been through for years and years and years. All we have to do is get him on that road and shepherd him down that whole process. Soon he'll be sitting in this chair when there's another new student sitting there, and he'll be one-upping him."

The example of relatable yet transformed peers has given TOSA a high success rate. TOSA hasn't seen one dirty drug test in its three years of operation. And the overall level of moral circumspection is astounding: scores of former criminals and hardcore meth and heroin addicts—men and women—living and working together, and no one is trying to game the system.

"Thirteen years my roommate's been out of prison and he's been nothing but a positive role model for me," Joe says. "Every night I come into that room he asks me how my day was, what's going on, and has nothing but positive things to tell me. If he can change his life, I believe I can change mine."

Time for transformation

"The short answer to why this works," Grenny says, "is because it's long and it's real. It allows you to stay in a mode of practicing new behaviors until they go to the marrow of your bone. Some people will stay at The Other Side Academy for four or five years, sometimes longer. But they stay as long as it takes until they get it, rather than until the funding runs out."

Grenny views most rehab as operating like a business transaction. "People will ask, 'How long is it going to take?' The answer comes back, 'Well, how much money do you have?' So they'll do a 30-day program because that's what the government will reimburse. Or 60 days, or 90 days. Let me tell you, if you've been in and out of jail your whole life, living on the street, 60 days is an insult."

Among other realities, TOSA students often struggle to accept the love that comes with the accountability. Running the streets for as long as many of them have, they don't know what it's like to truly be cared for. TOSA is their introduction to intimate connection.

Larry, who had decided to stay a third year in the program, says, "We have a guy who's on contract now" (that's when you break a rule and have to wear a yellow t-shirt which sets you apart for several days and prohibits you from speaking as you work alongside your peers), and "he said he preferred it. For him, contract helped him isolate himself"—which was familiar. "The hard part was people coming to him and saying, 'How are you doing?' and, 'You're gonna be all right,' and 'We got your back.' He said, 'Their care made me so uncomfortable. I'd rather they leave me alone.'" He wasn't ready for relationship and accountability.

Larry says that TOSA's patience relieves pressure for you to put on a false face of changed behavior. "They don't say, 'Time's up.' Or, 'we want to make room for other people.' They know what it takes to change someone like me."

Extended time not only allows moral transformation to occur, it also lets the habits of a productive life form. A crucial part of the TOSA formula is the businesses operated by students. They provide daily discipline, purpose, satisfaction, and lessons in self-reliance. And the funds they throw off pay for 80 percent of the organization's work. The other 20 percent comes from donations.

The first company started was The Other Side Movers. "Loading moving trucks allows people with very little skill to work hard and attend to detail," says Grenny. "It's an arduous job that leaves little time for people to ruminate and live in their heads—which is a dangerous place to be for the first few months after a person enters the TOSA regime. We teach everything from showing up on time, to packing cleanly, to sweeping the floor, and eventually to running the office side of the company."

In 2017, TOSA started a thrift store. When they move, many of the affluent households served by The Other Side Movers end up with clothing, furniture, dishes, and other items they would like to donate. The thrift operation makes that a seamless process. The store is clean, orderly, carries good products, and has attentive customer service. "It's more of an experience than a store," says a proud Susan.

> Business activity teaches students how to get up every day, go to work, have a good attitude, do as you're asked, learn how to learn, go to bed, and do it again the next day.

Students have also started a construction company and a landscaping firm, culinary services, and an autobody shop. Other students sit in the basement of the Academy's home for eight-hour shifts making calls and explaining the organization's mission to potential donors. It's not one particular set of skills that TOSA wants to develop. It's more concerned that you learn how to get up every day, go to work, have a good attitude, do as you're asked, learn how to learn, go to bed, and do it again the next day.

"You may not graduate from The Other Side Academy and go get a job at a moving company or restaurant. You may get a job at a place that you've always wanted to work prior to you destroying your life," says Durocher. "The idea is you can leave and be a success anywhere…that you gain some portable social capital."

So far, TOSA has produced 39 graduates, only one of whom has relapsed. About 25 percent of entrants to the program opt out during the 30-day orientation phase; beyond that point, they go the distance. Many graduates of the two-year program choose to stay on for a third (they're called master students). Those who graduate and leave are employed, drug-free, crime-free, and living productive, positive lives.

Bridge to the other side

After two or more years of hard work, brutal honesty, communal living, and gradual transformation, TOSA students get to a much vaunted day: Graduation. Like everything else at The Other Side, there's a physical monument marking the transition, in this case, a bridge that extends from the front door to the rest of their lives. When students are first admitted into the program, they are brought to this same east side of campus, where at the foot of the bridge they make solemn promises to join the community and accept help for a new life. Graduation marks a return to the bridge, this time facing a watching world.

As families look on, the ceremony includes letters to each graduate read aloud by other TOSA participants, a message from Grenny, and then a recitation of vows before crossing over the bridge into handshakes. "Scotty O., you have a been a rock for me over the last 18 months," says one burly student in his public message to the graduate. "There have been times here where I felt unimportant, lost, anxious and misunderstood, times when I needed clarity about certain crucial topics like family, love, connection, disordered thoughts.... Never once have you been at a loss for just the right words. You are authentic, talented, and beautiful. I love you, and I know that you love me. Your actions have shown it. Now, true to what we do here, I will pass on this gift of love and understanding to others."

It's a strange thing to watch men with shaved heads and pockmarked faces speak with such open emotion. Some of the watching students are contorting their facial muscles, either too moved to show it publicly, or daunted by their own personal journeys ahead.

Then today's graduate, Scotty, speaks.

Right before I came here, I found myself yet again in that situation where everything in my life was crumbling, and I was ruining lives and hurting people and doing a lot of horrible things. I really was tired of doing all that, but I didn't know what else to do. I didn't feel like I deserved to see the world. I wanted to die. I had already done 14 years of my life incarcerated, and I didn't want to keep doing it. So I wrote a letter after someone told me about this place. I didn't know what to expect, but I figured it was better than going to prison, and better than dying.

So I got here and I thought, this is the weirdest place ever. These people are nuts. All the staff members were nice and friendly, and then every once in a while they were really mean. It drove me nuts when I first got here. And then I realized that it was really *my* thoughts that were crazy. *My* view on things was so upside-down.

After being here for two years, I think the biggest thing that I have learned is that it is not about me. It's about the next guy and the newest guy. It's about finding somebody who needs help and helping them. And that's the only way that I get better. I learned that from Lola, and Dave, and all the staff here. It seems like they are always trying to help the next person. You know, from the small things, like seeing somebody stuck in the snow on the side of the road and just stopping whatever we are doing as a house and jumping up and helping them. Like I did when I was a little kid.

Scotty chokes up and pauses. "It's really nice now to be able to see myself as the kind of person who wants to give to the next guy, who wants to be there for people and be a good person."

Then Grenny speaks.

This here is what grace looks like. When you go to Florence and visit the famous David sculpture by Michelangelo, you're struck by how something so glistening and beautiful could be made from stone. You look at David's hand and you see veins on it. It literally looks like skin. That's what happens here. We take stones that are completely unshapen—often *mis*shapen—and…chisel each other…. It's a violent process. It involves really long, patient, aggressive activity. Scotty had to choose to stay here for two years, through 208 Games. That's a lot of chiseling, a lot of hammering…. Brothers and sisters here today, if you're feeling that violence and you don't like the feel of the chisel against you, just remember what you're on the way to becoming. Just remember what's at the end of that journey if you just choose to sit still. Because the way grace looks is that the chisel and hammer arrive, and the block of marble has to choose to accept the grace, to be willing to sit there and accept it.

Here Grenny tears up.

I watch that happening in this house every single day. Those of you that are deciding what to do in your third year, decide whether or not the chiseling is done, because there might be a little bit more work to do. For some, like Scotty, you'll make the decision for the chiseling to continue to happen out there, but with a tie to stay connected to the hammer's home base—us. So my question for the rest of you is: If you want to take control of your behavior, what do you have to do?

It's a question of context and moral norms.

All you've learned in the last two years is how to be people of character *here*. You haven't learned how to be this kind of person as a master's student or as a graduate student—you haven't learned that yet. So expect as soon as you cross that bridge, a whole new set of feelings and temptations and thoughts to start coming on. You have to stay connected to the exact same kind of influence structure that you've had here, to continue to become who you want to become. Stay still and let the chisel and the hammer continue to do its work. The worst thing you can do is start to feel entitled and say, "All right, I've done that. Now I get to enjoy life." No, you get to continue to be decent men and women, and that creates enjoyment.

Before he walks across the bridge to shake the hand of a previous graduate, now living as a free man, Scotty repeats a final vow: "I promise to show the world what TOSA is by having integrity and by being accountable. I promise to respond to any of my TOSA brothers or sisters in need. I promise to spend the rest of my life saving and serving others, just as you have saved and served me. Will you help me now as I do my best to live our beliefs on The Other Side?"

TOSA's staff, watching families, and the previous graduates respond, "Yes. You may now cross over."

Expanding ambitions

"I don't believe there's anything more important than the work we're doing," says Durocher. "Taking people and changing their lives, lives that they'd be utterly incapable of changing on their own. Providing a place that's safe to go, so they can get the help they need."

On more than one level, Durocher's conviction mirrors the crisis of the hour. Every year now, more than 70,000 of our citizens die of drug overdose—far more than the number of Americans who died during the

Vietnam War. Millions more suffer neglect or family breakdown because of substance abuse. As the *New York Times* reported in the investigative series "Addiction, Inc.," drug treatment has become one of the most lucrative health-care industries to emerge in a generation. There's an untapped market, and, because of that, an urgent need for institutions of integrity that put people before profit.

"The basic problem is not addiction," says Grenny. "The real problem is disconnection. People don't know how to live in an ordered, high-integrity, honest life with other people." TOSA's trying to change that, by helping residents practice decision-making until their intuitions are honed and shaped in healthy directions.

The gold standard that TOSA is setting really has two applications. The first involves franchising its model for addicts and criminals everywhere, and the second invites other professional sectors to apply the principles that undergird TOSA's success.

The Other Side Academy is currently raising funds to purchase 20 acres of land in Salt Lake City for the building of a model campus that could house 400-500 students. Leaders hope that 30 percent of the total funds necessary for this expansion will be granted by private donors. The remaining 70 percent they will seek as loans, to be paid off by revenues from the businesses run by TOSA students. "It's a wonderful symbol that the students get to say, 'We did twice as much as the community did,'" says Grenny. "And the community in turns says, 'We believed in you, and this is our way of saying that we're part of this, too.'"

The organization is also documenting all of its steps and processes so that its operations can be franchised in other cities. There are already donor commitments to bring the model to Denver (with Daniels Fund money), San Diego, and Chicago. A key issue both on the bigger Salt Lake City campus and in other cities will be maintaining the sense of community ownership that allows the program to work. Both Grenny and Durocher believe that to maintain intimacy and accountability, operating units need to be kept in the range of 100 students. Multiple units will operate in parallel to serve larger total numbers.

TOSA is also starting an entity to incubate companies owned and run by graduates, called UpSide Enterprises. The first business to be spun off by successful completers of the program will be a temp staffing and employment agency that works exclusively with people coming off the street or out of jail. "We figure our folks know how to mentor them better than anybody else," says Grenny. "And we believe it will be a profitable model"—because many cities face serious shortages today in manual-labor industries like construction and landscaping. "Plus we'll be offering a distinct quality of service experience."

Grenny's own business background will be a vital boost to these expansions. He was president of a successful IT company, then founded one of the most respected corporate training companies in the U.S. He has co-authored seven books on managing change, and products growing out of his research have been used to instruct more than 2 million workers.

TOSA isn't a traditional therapy or rehab operation. Officials don't know how to pigeonhole the nonprofit.

According to Grenny, the biggest challenge in expanding TOSA is, "Can we develop leaders fast enough? The critical component of our model is our leadership." The three people who run TOSA day in and day out—Dave Durocher, Lola Zagey, and Alan Fahringer—have a combined 45 years of experience with the Delancey Street model. TOSA is now developing a training regimen to turn some of its graduates into future Daves and Lolas. Candidates will begin as apprentices, then serve as junior staff, and eventually become full staff members. The program also wants to learn from other programs doing similar work, like Father Greg Boyle's Homeboy Industries in Los Angeles, and San Patrignano in Italy.

Grenny realizes that to attract donors, TOSA needs to be able to provide concrete measures of success. Compliance metrics like re-arrest numbers are easiest. Harder, yet more important in his view, are what he calls aspirational metrics. "Are graduates happy and connected and productive? Are they employed? Are they satisfied with their lives?"

TOSA aims to maintain contact with each graduate and track life satisfaction, financial health, relationship satisfaction, and other metrics as more graduates are produced, but it's tricky. "If somebody's messing up, they're not easy to get a hold of. So you have to be suspicious of data sets that say, 'Well we sent out a thousand surveys, we got 400 back, and here's the data from those 400.' We're trying to figure out how to solve that."

There are also regulatory minefields to navigate. TOSA isn't a traditional therapy or addiction-rehab operation. Officials don't know how to pigeonhole the nonprofit. Should the city zone them as a school? Monitor them as a drug program? Regulate them as a business? Treat them as a prisoner-reentry pathway? To keep itself free to make decisions as it deems best, TOSA so far hasn't taken a cent of government money.

And the group is zealously protecting the practices it considers crucial. "We will refuse ideas for expansion that expose us to infidelity to our model," says Grenny. "We've already run across some states that have laws that would be damaging to our operating procedures. We won't be going to those places."

Durocher and Grenny believe the model of accountability created by The Other Side Academy, and the nitty-gritty of its 12 operating beliefs, may also have wider value. "We recognize that we have this unique live-in community, but we think we can translate the principles that make it work beyond the criminal and addict profile. Corporate leaders seem increasingly to be clamoring for a new kind of culture, one defined by transparency and accountability. Maybe we can help."

Might TOSA's insights on moral accountability, peer-to-peer policing, learning by doing, and the value of rituals and physical monuments have value to companies, colleges, and other organizations? Spend a day at The Other Side Academy, and it hits you that the real world is so much softer, so mired in a spirit of victimization and individual rights to the exclusion of all else. TOSA is a beacon of counterculture, both in its communal nature and what it requires of each person to maintain it.

"I've learned more in the last two years about how to create a healthy, real community than I think I learned in the previous 28," says Grenny. His sentiments are reflected in the face of every other thriving student. "Look at how inappropriate all the boundaries are in every part of society today that we've seen with the whole #MeToo movement," says Tim Stay, one of TOSA's co-founders. "Both the participants and the surrounding environment were aware of what was going on, and yet no one was standing up and saying, 'Hey, this is inappropriate.'... Here there would be 50 people who would say, 'Whoa, you're not going into that room alone with that person. We know what kind of person he is.'"

Rare in this day and age, and even rarer given their histories, these students have come to *trust* this place. To trust its moral authority, its transformative alchemy, and even the pain such transformation requires. Critically, the trust is not just for the years they live and work as TOSA students, but for a way of being that is sufficient to direct the whole of one's life, and radiate outwards.

"What if our students—once felons and convicts—could show today's schools, corporations, and even religious institutions how to run an honest, trustworthy organization?" asks Grenny. "I think the reason our population is blessed is because they're so relatively broken. The problem with the rest of us is that we all are the same level of brokenness. And so we all think that, 'I guess it must be okay, because I am probably about as happy as he is and she is and she is.' So rather than asking the most important question in life, 'How good can I stand it?,' we settle for, 'Eh, this is probably about how it is.'"

You don't need to be a thief or an addict to be persuaded by the beauty of a solid moral compass. There's an opportunity for philanthropists to catch TOSA's vision and evangelize its approach: Physical monuments, rituals, peer-to-peer accountability, learning by doing, patience.

"I think all of us want this kind of intimacy," says Grenny. "It is what we are…we crave it. We just don't know how to do it."

Maybe this community of reformed rascals can lead the way.

A Contagion of Caring, One Block at a Time
Community Renewal International
Shreveport, Louisiana

"Light, light, more light!" they tell us the dying Goethe cried.
No. Warmth, warmth, more warmth! For we die of cold and not of darkness.
It is not the night that kills, but the frost.
~ Miguel de Unamuno, The Tragic Sense of Life

One of the most successful character initiatives in the country doesn't actually talk about character. Not up front, at least. Rather, the mission of a transformative organization based in Shreveport, Louisiana, is to revive neighborhoods and cities by restoring relationships—home by home, block by block.

In 1970, Rosie Chaffold moved to Shreveport from Bastrop, Louisiana. She was looking for a neighborhood with good schools and churches, and she specifically wanted "a rural philosophy, where people could pretty much know each other and look out for each other, and your children will do what I tell them to do and my children would do what you tell them to do."

Miss Rosie, as she's now called, found what she was looking for in a working-class black neighborhood called Allendale. At the time, Allendale had a mix of homes, businesses, restaurants, and congregations. Tina Turner and James Brown graced its music halls. For the first 15 years of her life there, despite unrest throughout the South, Allendale was exactly what she'd hoped for. "Students went to school, adults went to work, and families went to church. Children played with one another. We could leave our doors unlocked. It was wonderful."

But by the mid-1980s, many of the children who had grown up in Allendale were going off to college or the military and moving to the suburbs. Homeowners began to rent out their properties. "The people who came in to rent, they didn't have the same philosophy that the ones had when I first came," says Miss Rosie. "They came with a different point of view."

Allendale began to slide. At first, it was just a messy house here, an act of un-neighborliness there. But soon people started averting their eyes on the street, locking their doors, and hunkering down as one block sprouted six crack houses, and gun shots became routine. An interstate was built that cut off the neighborhood from the rest of Shreveport. Before long, Allendale was "pitiful. I actually felt ashamed to see something so beautiful go down so quick."

The deterioration of the neighborhood was linked to a deterioration of behavior. In the healthy Allendale there had been a moral ecology that nurtured traits like trust, self-discipline, and neighborly care. But that ecology got pushed aside. Marriage rates plummeted. Children grew up without fathers or loving attachment from neighbors and extended family. As isolation increased, so did drug use and the murder rate. In 1991 there were 80 homicides in Allendale—

almost two killings per week. Many people were living with the psychic trauma of dead loved ones. Before long, every single business in Allendale had closed or moved away. Residents saw little future for themselves.

Meanwhile, the larger city of Shreveport seemed uninterested. Legally, segregation was over, but whites weren't touching the city's black neighborhoods. An ethos of privacy and gated communities crept in. Wealthier kids shifted from local Little Leagues to travel teams and cultural exposures far away. Adults lost touch with their neighbors. City parks and playing fields grew fallow with disuse.

A man named Mack McCarter saw all this and was dismayed. A Shreveport native and proud alum of Byrd High School, he'd gone off to become a civil-rights activist in the late 1960s before heading to Texas for seminary and the pastorate. When he returned to Shreveport in 1991, he was shocked by the state of things. A reader of historian Arnold Toynbee, McCarter realized he wasn't just seeing a city in a tailspin, he was watching a whole culture decline.

It kept McCarter up at night. He refused to accept that doom was inevitable. He knew he had to do something to stem the tide.

"If society is fundamentally relational," McCarter says, "then, from what I'd learned from thousands of hours of pastoral counseling, society could be healed." Decades of walking alongside people struggling with broken marriages, abuse, familial dysfunction, and loneliness convinced McCarter that relationships have rules—rules that are "just as ineluctable as the laws of gravity."

McCarter wrote up some of his observations. Community life starts in acquaintances, fueled by simple conversation. After repeated sharing of ideas and opinions, these eventually grow into friendships. Finally, deeper convictions and feelings are shared, producing an intimacy that makes people more vulnerable and more interlinked and trusting, which McCarter calls partnership.

McCarter thought an organization could coach people to develop healthy relationships. He sketched a set of simple rules:

- You must seek the other person's good just as you seek your own.
- Other people are never to be used as a means, but treasured for their own sake.
- Forgive all wounds to the mind, emotions, or spirit, whether slight or serious.

- Confess your own wounding actions, and seek forgiveness.
- Give the other person attention, aiming always to deepen and sustain the relationship.

The pastor stared hard at these principles and wondered what they would look like if applied to a whole city. He had a suspicion that most anti-poverty and social-improvement efforts were undermined by a failure to build the healthy relationships they require—relationships that were the necessary foundation for things like safety, good neighboring, and motivated workers.

McCarter came up with a formula: Build community first, teach the skills of caring, and walk the talk with simple acts. Once people realize the power of relationships, he hypothesized, they can move their communities to higher levels of well-being.

> Community Renewal revives neighborhoods and cities by restoring relationships—home by home, block by block.

The power of personalism

Mack McCarter set out to test his hypothesis in Allendale—which had by then become the poorest and most dangerous neighborhood in Shreveport. Every Saturday morning, McCarter would drive to Allendale, park his car, and simply walk the blocks. He didn't come with an agenda; he came with curiosity, and the sentiment was reciprocated. Who was this tall white man who extended hugs with warm winks and self-deprecating jokes? Why did he keep returning every weekend?

Allendale's children were the first to leap over the sidewalk shyness, following McCarter in a pied-piper parade. Parents began to observe warily, cracking open their windows and stepping onto porches to see who this visitor was. Awkward "How do you do" conversations began, followed by tentative steps toward familiarity and friendship.

"I was suspicious of Mack at first," recalls Miss Rosie. "I didn't want him to know me. I didn't want to be let down. I had been disappointed by other people who claimed they wanted to do something for Allendale, yet accomplished nothing."

But McCarter kept showing up. He and his wife joined Allendale's Baptist church, the two white faces in the pews. Neighborhood residents started to sit out on their front porches at the hours when they knew the couple would come strolling. Even the drug dealers were disarmed by his guileless nature. Everyone warmed to his attentiveness and good humor. "There was something about his speaking that sounded sincere," Miss Rosie recalls.

After two years of consistent presence, McCarter created a training workshop for people interested in building stronger relationships with their neighbors. He knew that the insiders would have more legitimacy than he or any other well-intentioned white outsider could earn. Commissioned "Haven House leaders," participants would be taught how to befriend others on their block. They would be responsible for organizing neighborhood gatherings, staying abreast of needs and crises within the community, and encouraging a spirit of openness and generosity.

"We're remaking our city by making friends on our street," said McCarter. That became the motto of the Haven House plan.

It was a modest beginning. But fast-forward two decades, and major crime in Allendale is down 60 percent, the drug dealers are gone, former gang leaders have become block coordinators, and neighbors stroll comfortably from one house to the next. Kids play outdoors, and grandmothers tend tomatoes in the "Allendale Garden of Hope & Love." There are two residential community centers called Friendship Houses that provide tutoring, food, and character-building experiences for kids, high-school-equivalency test training, family support, and other help. The neighborhood's self-image has improved, and property values have appreciated.

"The best thing that could happen to Allendale was seeing the people come together as a group," states Lee Jeter. He's a former marine who runs Shreveport's chapter of the Fuller Center for Housing (created by the same couple who founded Habitat for Humanity, Millard and Linda Fuller), which builds and repairs houses in partnership with families in need. "People now say, 'This is our community, and we're going to take charge.' If you can take a place that was in decline and decay like Allendale, and revitalize it from the inside, then…it can happen in any community in the United States."

Allendale's revival has inspired replications in other parts of Shreveport, including Highland, Cedar Grove, Queensborough, and the Barksdale Annex in neighboring Bossier. One sees in each place the same striking improvements in safety, resident satisfaction, educational trajectories, and personal transformation. Some affluent pockets of Shreveport have also joined in, unlocking their doors and rediscovering the joys of knowing one's neighbors.

McCarter's goal is to "re-villagize the city," and it starts with a simple yet powerful principle: Make visible that which is already going on, namely, caring acts by caring individuals.

Community Renewal, the nonprofit that grew out of McCarter's core insight, created a "We Care" initiative that asks residents to sign cards where they describe one thing they're doing to help someone else. It might be taking communion to a disabled person from church. It might be something as simple as regularly sweeping debris off a neighbor's walkway. In exchange for filling out the card, you get a lapel pin, a bumper sticker, and a yard sign bearing the words We Care. It is a stamp of membership that is now recognized across the city—54,500 residents now consider themselves part of the We Care team—shared across boundaries of neighborhood, race, and economic circumstance.

This is a simple, affirming way to boost the better angels already at work in a community. The We Care signs bolster the ranks of doers who are generous and attuned to their neighbors. They serve as signals to help caring people learn of one another's existence, and connect. Over time, an organic, volunteer-driven caring network emerges, sparking unlikely friendships and enabling residents to feel like they belong to something greater than themselves.

"Seeing the familiar We Care sign in a yard on the opposite side of town changes the whole psychological dimension of how you might otherwise feel in an alien environment," says McCarter. "There is now a commonality that runs from the retired university president to somebody walking the street in Allendale. They share a mutual concern and commitment. It's powerful."

Community Renewal's goal is to expand the number of people participating in the We Care initiative from the current 54,500 to 130,000. Already, the bumper stickers, lapel pins, and yard flags are very visible across this city of 300,000. It may sound soft, but in Shreveport, caring has become a unifying identity, shifting perceptions of a city known for crime and segregation into a community increasingly knit together by shared goals, shared responsibilities, and mutual moral improvement.

"I met Mack and everything changed," says Paige Hoffpauir, a leader in Southern Trace, a gated community and the wealthiest, whitest neighborhood in Shreveport. "When I was drawn into Community Renewal's work, I realized *I* was the charity. I used to be a person who had no time to talk to people. If it didn't directly benefit me, and quickly, I saw no reason for relationship building or any of that. But when I started walking with Community Renewal, absorbed the paradigm, and started acting on some of the steps, I began to get unlocked."

> Competent, compassionate, whole people don't spring up on their own. They grow up out of relationships.

McCarter suggests that competent, compassionate, whole people don't spring up on their own. They grow up out of relationships. "We won't have strong individual character unless we have a community that's conducive to it," he says firmly. "The cancer is disconnection. We need reconnection. Our job at Community Renewal is not to create yet another nonprofit to deliver services. Rather, our job is to build a platform of mutually enhancing relationships, relationships that draw out each individual's best, and to nourish that living platform for all of us."

Everyone who's been involved in this intentional caring network testifies to incredible transformation on both personal and communal levels. People across the socioeconomic spectrum report a rediscovery of life purpose. Residents describe the game-changer it's been to know and be known by one's neighbors. And citizens at large feel empowered to contribute from their unique talents, to serve as hosts, bridge-builders, entrepreneurs, and community healers.

"It is important that people recognize that caring people outnumber those who are not," McCarter says. "We want to make visible what is already real. Catastrophe will do that. It will strip off the veneer. 9/11 didn't change people in New York City. It revealed them."

Villagize the city

A second big part of Community Renewal's strategy is the Haven House. It takes the We Care interest in "coordinated neighboring" and adds structure and accountability. Volunteers willing to make their home a Haven House serve as hubs for the mutual care of 20 other residences on their street. They bring neighbors together through simple initiatives like block parties, taking meals to sick neighbors, helping find lost pets, mowing yards, sending birthday cards, picking up newspapers for each other, or just offering a sympathetic ear. The effort could be thought of as a way of re-creating in a city the intimate knowledge and mutual responsibility of a small town.

Leaders are encouraged to creatively apply McCarter's "Rules of Relationships" to the needs of their own community. They get tips and training on how to overcome social fears, ideas for outreach, and a strong network of support. Haven House leaders meet monthly in groups of 20 with a coordinator to document progress in building relationships, share best practices, and solve problems.

"How do we get people to do this?" one Haven House leader asks rhetorically. "Well, you have to give a vision. Remind people what it used to be like. For instance, I sometimes say something like, 'When I grew up, we all knew each other.' People respond, 'Yeah, that's right.' I say, 'Nobody on my street, when I grew up, had a burglar alarm. If somebody had said they were installing a burglar alarm we would have thought they were crazy. Or hiding gold.' People nod. 'Now, we set our burglar alarms without even thinking about it. That is disintegration at its base level.' People are in tune with you at that point. And then I say, 'So how do we solve this? The only way is to get reconnected.' "

Recruiting the right kind of Haven House leader is crucial. It needs to be someone who is already respected in the neighborhood, who is kind, open, and willing to be available when needs flare at an inconvenient time.

There are strict prohibitions against any agenda other than building friendships. Haven House leaders aren't allowed to put up political yard signs. Fundraising is a no-no. "I don't care if it's heart disease or cancer research," McCarter says, "we are radical on these things. We've had years of lack of trust, so how do we overcome that? There are certain things we have to do and not do."

The kind of extroversion that Community Renewal equips its Haven House leaders to encourage in their neighborhoods isn't for everyone.

With residents who are suspicious, the Haven House leader is trained to stay friendly but not push. The hope is that at some point one neighbor will develop a relationship with the skeptic next door and melt away barriers, little by little. The ultimate goal is to shift the neighborhood ecology away from radical privacy and autonomy and toward sharing and caring, so trust and goodwill become second nature.

"You begin to understand that when we know our neighbors, it's a lot more fun to live where you live," says a Haven House leader who's been at it for eight years. "It's also safer. And easier. If you have a toilet that's overflowing and you don't know what to do, you can call next door. Or if you lose your dog. When we know people, we reach out."

There are now more than 1,500 trained Haven House block leaders in greater Shreveport. Each does something a little different. Some sponsor neighborhood caroling or cookie exchanges during the holiday season. One organized a youth car wash to buy school supplies for students in Allendale. Another gathered the neighborhood's elderly residents for regular blood-pressure measuring and walks. Some have coordinated with the police to start a Neighborhood Watch. Others ask local businesses to sponsor them with garbage bags, gloves, and pick-up sticks for quarterly neighborhood clean-ups.

Some Haven House leaders publish a block directory. Others find someone to create and distribute a monthly newsletter, with photos and information about people's health, family updates, crime news, and community-wide events. Every leader makes it a priority to learn the names and occupations of all those on his or her block, and everyone is encouraged to research the history of the neighborhood. "There will be no better group of people that knows the passions, the desires, the hurts of the people across a city than Haven House at full scale," says Kim Mitchell, director of Community Renewal's lab for national replication.

One Haven House leader invited the youth on her block to interview senior adults. Then a picnic was held where older residents taught the children bygone games like Kick the Can, Jacks and Marbles, and Hopscotch. "There are a million different and inventive ways to meet our neighbors," says Haven House coordinator Russell Minor. "There's not one way. We're just providing a system and coordination."

In loco parentis

Community Renewal's third strategy is the Friendship House. Volunteer contractors and contributing partners build houses with a large common room and a big front porch, each in a low-income, high-crime area. Trained staff and their families live in these Friendship Houses and work with local children and adults, providing educational assistance, mentoring, life skills, conflict resolution, parent training, and family support. Ten Friendship Houses currently operate, and they have already served more than 3,500 children.

Walk up to the Allendale Friendship House today, and you'll find the neighborhood kids participating in a local drill team led by husband and wife Emmitt and Sharpel Welch, the resident house counselors. The kids are uniformed and march in formation, singing and chanting. They reel off the books of the Bible in unison, looks of steely concentration in their eyes. After years in the Army, the Welches know how to build discipline and concentration. But it took them a while to fuel local participation.

> There are more than 1,500 Haven House leaders creatively caring in Shreveport. Some sponsor caroling, others organize a car wash to buy school supplies, or make a block directory.

"When I first got to Allendale," recalls Emmitt, "I was meeting 17-year-old kids who couldn't look at a clock on the wall and tell you what time it was. Who didn't know how to tie a shoe. I was blown away. At first I was looking at them like something strange out of a horror movie, and they were looking at me basically the same way. Word on the street was that I was a narcotics agent. They were showing up and eating my pizza, but they were told by their peers: 'Don't give Emmitt any information.' They weren't even telling me their names."

Then "something strange happened. You know, when love is given out, love has got to come back in. These kids began to come around. The parents were peeping through the windows into the Friendship House. They began to put the message out, 'This guy is for real.' "

Now, "when they come up those stairs, I make sure that I look them in the face to see if their heads are slumped down and they're kicking rocks, or if their heads are held up high and they're running in here. If they're running in here, we're going to have a pretty good day. If their head is hung down, that means we had trouble at home and we're going to have trouble today."

Welch explains that "we put conditions in their lives. We tell them there are standards. Little things as well as big things. We tell them they are responsible for cleaning up around this place. They are responsible for being nice and courteous to one another."

The first year I was here, we spent most of our time at the principal's office, down at the sheriff's office. Dealing with alcohol. Going to juvenile hall and taking handcuffs off the kids who were locked until someone picked them up. All that stuff. We start telling them that this is totally unacceptable behavior. That we have standards we expect of you (which, by the way, is what the parents should have been doing).

We offered a welding program. Activities to keep them busy. Guess what started happening? The grades started coming up. We stopped going to the principal's office. Nobody had cared enough to tell these kids that there is a standard we must live by. But if you put a level of expectancy in these kids' minds, let them know what you expect out of them, if you give them a hug and let them know you're proud of them, these kids will go 110 percent for you.

Emmitt and Sharpel try to widen the horizons of these young people. "Some of our kids had never been to the state capitol. I loaded them all in the van and we took them down to Government Plaza, walked around, prayed, and came back. I got permission to take them down to Space Center Houston a couple years ago. First time they'd ever left Shreveport. Last year at spring break, we took all the kids to San Antonio. On these trips, they're in a place they don't recognize, where they don't know anyone, and the only thing they have to latch onto is each other and the standard of excellence that we put on them."

Friendship House leaders like the Welches try to involve all those willing to be part of coaxing and encouraging the young. Once a month, they have a family night where everyone in the neighborhood is invited to a large barbecue. Folks get to know each other, shake hands, and talk about what's happening in and around Allendale.

"Some people say we're substitute parents," says Emmitt. "I call it standing in the gap, doing whatever is necessary to keep this thing together. I tell the kids when they come in here, it doesn't matter if your last name is Jones, Jackson, or Williams. We're all family. We're not going to attack each other. We're going to love each other, and we're going to do the very best we can. If we don't love them, and if we don't reach out to them, some of these kids are going to grow up to be monsters. But if you just keep rubbing on a jagged edge, it's going to become smooth after a while. It's a process, but we're getting it done."

Mutual reinforcement, and an ambition to scale

From these three overlapping efforts—the We Care initiative, the Haven House network, and the Friendship Houses in the toughest neighborhoods—have grown all sorts of sub-initiatives. There is now the Adult Renewal Academy, which helps people earn their GED and find gainful employment, while honing their parenting skills and connecting themselves to a larger support network. There's a sewing apprenticeship program for women. There are summer camp offerings that allow kids from neighborhoods like Allendale to experience nature in Missouri.

A group of teenage women called Girl Pearls meets twice a month with a set of older female mentors who orchestrate candid discussions of self-esteem, abuse, race, sexuality, identity. One of the leaders was tired of seeing teenage pregnancies at the end of every summer, so she gave each girl a golden egg and made her responsible for a regimen of dressing and feeding it, carrying it everywhere, and putting it to sleep. It was an exercise in the responsibilities of parenting, and by the end "those girls were so tired of their eggs! They didn't want to see them again!"

Community Renewal answers two key questions for donors keen to advance character-forming conditions across the country. First, can social capital be repaired intentionally? The message of studies like Robert Putnam's *Bowling Alone* is that social capital just grows up naturally and is hard to replace once stripped away. But Community Renewal suggests that links among neighbors can be regrown, even in the face of corrosive factors like gangs, drugs, economic pressure, and racial baggage.

The second question is: Can character formation happen in groups? We all know of individual character programs. But can you create a whole moral ecology in which it is easier to be good, which nurtures kindness, compassion, accountability, and personal responsibility?

Community Renewal is proving that you can. It gives people social roles (We Care member, Haven House leader, community coordinator,

Friendship House parent, etc.) that provide individuals with a sense of responsibility, dignity, belonging, and agency. It anoints norm-setters who hold up and enforce standards of locally acceptable behavior. It creates accountability mechanisms for people to keep refining their behavior. It decentralizes initiative and responsibility, so that most activity is intimate rahter than impersonal—often limited to a couple dozen households. It creates positive feedback loops: Healthy community inspires wholesome habits, improved behavior, better people, better communities. And all this is not charity and dependency but local control and responsibility.

Many donors have given to Community Renewal, though few have made sustained investments over the long haul. It's been hard for the group to communicate its successes. "How do you quantify love?" muses Floyd Morris, who helped steer some Robert Wood Johnson Foundation money to Community Renewal when he was a program officer. "How do you put that down in words and not have people look at you as some idealistic kook?"

The organization's focus on building and sustaining relationships over a long period of time doesn't readily align with expectations for shorter term, concrete outcomes that many foundations and corporate social responsibility teams now require. Paul Ellingstad, who guided some of Hewlett Packard's corporate philanthropy to Community Renewal, explains: "The benefits and the social value an organization like Community Renewal creates in the long run can't be reduced to a typical corporate dashboard of performance indicators and evaluated in the same way." He says that "Mack thinks and works to enable loving, caring communities that thrive across generations—not quarters."

Morris, who now leads an organization in Trenton, New Jersey, called Children's Futures, reports that when he first encountered Community Renewal back in the mid-1990s, "I couldn't believe something like this actually existed. I started reading about the process of relationship, and connection, and people coming together to build social capital. There was one section that talked about a Friendship House being built in the most difficult area of Shreveport, with that home being used for job training, after-school programs, family training, neighbor to neighbor. It all resonated."

He went down to Louisiana to see it in the flesh. "They had a training process. They were connecting people with people they trusted, institutions they trusted. They had an ability to dialogue around issues like drug use and crime. It was and is the soft stuff, but it's what makes the world go 'round." The Robert Wood Johnson Foundation first fronted $400,000 and ultimately provided $2,635,583, much of it aimed at building up the research capacity of Community Renewal so that expansion would eventually be possible.

In 2000, architect and city planner Kim Mitchell began experimenting with the potential of the Community Renewal model to transform cities. In 2014, after a successful 40-year career, Mitchell retired from his firm to become the founding director of the Center for Community Renewal. Its role is to create and track data streams demonstrating effects, as well as to map out strategies for expanding the Shreveport model to other places. Currently nine U.S. cities are in various phases of replicating the model, and this ambition has begun to attract potential donors. In 2015, the Avedis Foundation studied Shreveport's results and invested $1 million to front a year's worth of operation in its hometown of Shawnee, Oklahoma. Three years in, Shawnee is far ahead of schedule.

"The essential challenge [of our time] is to transform the isolation and self-interest within our communities into connectedness and caring for the whole." These are the words of Peter Block, author of the 2008 book *Community: The Structure of Belonging*. Insofar as this is right, what disciplines bring tools to measure isolation and self-interest, connectedness and caring? Could such measurements win the philanthropic support that Community Renewal and other transformative character efforts need? Better yet, could legitimate measurements of the "softer" substrate of a flourishing society help design a methodology that could be franchised or licensed, so the program isn't beholden to restricted grants? Or do donors simply need to pay more attention to the conditions that make for healthy relationships in the first place, forestalling measurement for practical (and principled) know-how?

For now Community Renewal is working on establishing a leadership institute to train social entrepreneurs from around the world in the model and send them to places as far-flung as Cameroon and Minneapolis, Abilene, and Washington, D.C.

"Caring alone cannot heal our nation," says McCarter. "But caring together can."

Educating the
Whole Person
Wake Forest University
Winston-Salem,
North Carolina

The great use of life is to spend it for something that outlasts it.
~ William James

"If you haven't been to a college campus in the last six years, you don't understand how radically the atmosphere has changed," commented New York University psychologist Jonathan Haidt recently. He was speaking in the aftermath of the 2017 attack on Charles Murray at Middlebury College, where a mob of students obstructed Murray's speech and then violently drove the social scientist off campus, injuring the professor escorting him, and doing property damage in the process. It was a disturbing incident in a series of campus frenzies caught up in a wave of moral ultimatums on the way history should be told, narratives of oppression and victimhood, and a capitulation to the therapeutic as the only way to make sense of truth.

These ultimatums have coincided with an avalanche of gender identity, discrimination, and sexual-assault claims on college campuses, the #MeToo movement, and a renewed reckoning with the nation's racial sins. Technology and a heightened sense of social pressure have worsened the mental health of our young adults. In all this, one sees a generation coming of age without guide or guardrail, floundering to direct its moral yearnings with maturity, and institutions at a loss as to how to help them.

The results are troubling. Nationwide, 11.5 percent of college students say they contemplated suicide in 2018 (from 6 percent in 2007); 66 percent reported binge drinking in the past two weeks (from 43 percent in 2007); 33 percent are on medication for depression or anxiety (from 20 percent in 2007). As measured on the Diener Flourishing Scale, only 45 percent of college undergraduates were thriving in 2016, according to the Healthy Minds Network survey.

Beneath these foreboding indicators, a foundational question is resurfacing: *What is college education for?* Is it for learning and teaching, or is it for faculty research? Should it be an agent of social mobility, or even social engineering? Is it about training people for the labor market, or is it about forming them into active citizens and mature human beings?

The answers are shifting as the landscape changes. Today, the bulk of jobs requiring a bachelor's degree increasingly demand "soft" skills like collaboration, empathy, the ability to read a complex situation and deftly navigate its subtler demands. As more jobs are being replaced by automation, there's a recognition that universities can no longer be sources of information alone; rather, they need to be incubators of relational skills, highly integrative analytical capacities, and agile leadership.

At the same time, students themselves are exhausted by the "achievatron" mentality that's driven many of their upbringings. Rather than it being a bridge between adolescence and adulthood, most understand college to be yet one more competition for advancement. Too many campuses now are characterized by anxiety and a scramble for status, not the shared quest for truth that's historically grounded the university's telos.

Libraries could be stocked with books explaining the cause of this fraught climate on America's campuses, but at the center is a moral void. The humane lessons offered by great literature and art are less taught and less learned. Ruthless social media and credentialing hierarchies have created artificial expectations and increased peer pressures. Declining religious practice has cut students off from spiritual support. The modern university, laments former Harvard dean Harry Lewis in his book *Excellence Without a Soul*, has forgotten Emerson's conclusion that the honing of the mind can be pernicious if not paired with the development of character.

> According to a 2016 Veritas Forum student survey, "developing a coherent worldview" is the thing students most want to accomplish in college.

Some within academia are trying to correct the course. Organizations like the Hyde Park Institute at the University of Chicago, the Lyceum Fellows at Clemson University, and the Veritas Forum at Ivy League and other top-tier schools aim to offer students deeper modes of inquiry into truth and the moral commitments they will make in life. The Agora Institute at Johns Hopkins and St. Olaf's Institute for Freedom & Community aim to foster the virtues of good citizenship. There are numerous programs that champion the Great Books and the study of history and evolved wisdoms. Most of these start-ups are respectful of religion and tradition, operating as close-knit communities that recognize that deep formation happens best when people are committed to the growth of one another and the pursuit of great ideas and noble action, one day at a time.

Students are flocking. Yale's "Life Worth Living" course now attracts 150 applications for only 40 slots. "Justice" with Harvard's Michael Sandel enrolls 1,115 students. According to a 2016 Veritas Forum student survey, "developing a coherent worldview" is the thing students most want to accomplish in college. In a recent Dartmouth College spirituality survey, 88 percent of respondents said they were on a "spiritual quest," and 78 percent said opportunities for spiritual growth are an essential or important part of college.

One school that is responding to these developments with sensitivity and ambition is Wake Forest University in Winston-Salem, North Carolina. Baptist by denominational heritage and led by the religious historian and former Notre Dame provost Nathan Hatch, Wake is now a top-30 secular institution that places a special emphasis on cultivating the whole person—head, heart, and helping hand—across every facet of the university. The school is intensely humanistic as it innovates on this question: "How do we train leaders not just to make a living, but to live?"

People first, programs second

It begins with the people, starting with President Hatch himself. "Character is the most pressing issue of our day, and one that institutions of higher education struggle to address," Hatch says. "We can far more easily study and talk about virtue and the good life than actually nurture character in the lives of students."

Hatch consistently cites Wake's motto, *Pro Humanitate,* as his animating principle. Translated "For Humanity," it is an exhortation toward selfless living, reclaiming education as the quest to explore what it is to be human, across time and in particular contexts. "I relish that opportunities abound at Wake Forest for students to serve and to be challenged by the big questions," Hatch said in his opening university address in 2005. "What can I know? In what can I believe? To what should I be committed?" He has since wrapped just about every possible program—academic and extracurricular—in these questions.

But instead of reforming by-laws, he's hired people. "It all has to do with the right person," Hatch is fond of saying. Wake's career services office was one of the first places he focused on.

Andy Chan was at Stanford's Business School during the dot-com boom of the 1990s, and remembers how easy it was to get jobs. Yet something about that era seemed unsustainable. He wanted to help students make more thoughtful choices about their work and futures. He read Jim Collins's *Built to Last* about long-term versus flash-in-the-pan business successes, and began experimenting with ways to transfer that book's lessons to personal career choices.

"At the time, there wasn't appetite for a deeper conversation around career and vocation," Chan recalls. Less than 10 percent of the faculty at Stanford responded to his initiative. Then Chan learned about the Lilly Endowment's work in fostering opportunities for vocational discernment among college students, and started experimenting. Instead of simply having students take self-diagnostic tests in isolation and then feeding them to recruiters, Chan created a course called Career & Life Vision, and made it a requirement for Stanford's first-year business students. It exploded.

"Students are in a lot of pain to figure out their way," Chan says. Beneath the pragmatic choice of this path versus that path, "there are deep questions of who they are."

President Hatch got wind of Stanford's course and its success. He wooed Chan to do something similar at Wake Forest. Chan reflects, "At Wake I saw a leader and a school more favorable to integrating personal development with career development. Only the top person—in this case the college president—can ask people to aspire to be their best selves." Shortly after he arrived, Chan raised $5 million from 30 families so he could fund new initiatives at Career Services without siphoning money away from Wake's academic departments.

That was nine years ago. Career Services has since been renamed the Office of Personal and Career Development and has become a standard-bearer for this kind of work. The keystone is a set of "College-to-Career" courses that have Wake students reading psychology, philosophy, and history, and even studying chess, together meant to crystallize their questions about what and who to serve after graduating. There are reinforcing discussions, reflection exercises, experiments, and apprenticeships, many of them taking place within mentoring relationships with faculty or alumni.

Chan is now helping other institutions build their own college-to-career bridge. He emphasizes Wake's distinctive element of requiring coursework. The seminar element is indispensable to getting students to grapple with the questions of meaning, purpose, and commitment-making that will eventually pervade their lives.

"Most students walk into a career-services office to get something done in 30 minutes. They approach us in fix-it terms: 'I just want to end this anxiousness.' And the job of typical college career officers is to get students internships and jobs. Most can't conceive of adding yet one more task. So you *have* to sit students down in a course. It's the only way to get them to think about this" from all the angles they'll need for purposeful lives.

Another one of President Hatch's key hires was Steve Reinemund, former CEO of PepsiCo, who served as dean of Wake Forest's business school from 2008 to 2014. Hatch and Reinemund had known each other for some years through shared service on the national board of Salvation Army. Then Hatch asked the executive to fix serious problems at the business school. "For the most part I believe academics are better suited to lead academic institutions," says Reinemund. "But sometimes tough business decisions are best made by outsiders."

A graduate of the Naval Academy and a longtime trustee at Chick-fil-A and Walmart, Reinemund was as passionate about personal formation as Hatch, and made this the cornerstone of Wake's business education. Arriving right after the national mortgage meltdown, Lehman Brothers collapse, and other failures of the Great Recession, he articulated a new mission for the school: "Developing passionate, ethical business leaders driven to achieve results with integrity." The new curriculum and mentoring scheme emphasized fostering character and principled behavior along with competence. In 2014, Wake shifted away from the traditional, daytime program to serve working professionals in the evenings, becoming the #1 part-time MBA program in North Carolina.

Bringing character into new academic departments

Even before the financial crisis, Reinemund notes, business schools were likelier than other departments of higher education to emphasize the pragmatic importance of character. Almost all b-schools, for instance, provided training in "leadership." But in the last decade, he argues, students have "clamored for questions of character to take a more active role in their business education." He says smart leaders now realize they can't succeed in this area simply by tightening compliance rules. Instead, character training and moral responsibility need to be infused into each aspect of their companies, enchanting the institutional mission itself.

Wake Forest promotes the idea that good character is built through repeated quotidian choices, solidified long before dramatic tests arise. This approach attracted another moral gardener to campus: Michael Lamb. Raised on a small family farm in Tennessee, Lamb earned academic and service scholarships to attend Rhodes College in Memphis, where a particularly profound course entitled "Hunger, Plenty, and Justice" sparked an interest in integrating academic study with community service.

Lamb's college scholarship required ten hours of volunteer labor per week. He initially viewed this as a way of paying his tuition. But, as he reflected in a later essay, "working at soup kitchens, building Habitat houses, and tutoring elementary students transformed how I saw myself and the world. I began to see the difference between *doing community service* and *serving the community*. Service, I realized, wasn't merely a collection of one-time projects or a way to build a résumé; it was a way of life that pervades all that we are and all that we do."

Lamb went on to become a Rhodes Scholar, Princeton doctoral student, and dean of leadership, service, and character development for the Rhodes Trust at Oxford University. He was recruited to Wake Forest in 2016, where Hatch asked him to build a path-breaking program in character and leadership training. Despite the many "ethics" initiatives at universities today, "few translate that work to the actual formation of student leaders," says Hatch. Given Wake Forest's own history and identity, he hopes its programming could offer a model of how to do this for other colleges and universities." Certainly "there has never been more interest in forming leaders of character, given the crisis of leadership evident in civic life, in the professions, and in business—but almost no one has a real plan for how to do this."

Lamb did have a plan. He and his team at the Oxford Character Project had developed "Ethics Through Fiction and Film" reading groups to help students use novels and films to expand their moral imagination. They organized a "Portraits of Leaderships" tour at the National Portrait Gallery to consider how artists can shape one's vision of leadership. They recruited a jazz professor to help students think about what the genre can teach about leading and following, improvising and collaborating. They invited a Shakespeare scholar to lead a conversation on leadership after viewing *King Lear*. Oxford students had responded hungrily to these kinds of opportunities. They snatched up opportunities to probe the deeper "whys" beneath their rigorous tenure as Rhodes Scholars.

Now Lamb intends to do something similar at Wake Forest. "Often, when we think of 'leaders,' we think of 'heroic' leaders, the one person out in front—the politician, the general, the CEO, the person who holds a position of institutional authority and exercises command and control. These leaders are important, but they are not the only kind of leaders. And they are not the kind of leaders that millennials tend to follow or become.... Therefore, we will focus on developing and teaching new models of everyday leadership."

Most leadership programs focus on teaching students how to run a meeting, delegate authority, or communicate effectively. "These skills are necessary," says Lamb, "but they're not sufficient. After all, leaders can use their skills for either good or ill. Our program will teach our students to be not just *effective* leaders, but *ethical* leaders."

It will emphasize both individual virtues and community contributions. "Many civic engagement programs at other places focus on only community service without explicitly exploring how character shapes community and how community shapes character. We will focus on both." And all kinds of students will be pulled in. "Much of the recent discourse on leadership has been confined to business or management.... Our liberal arts tradition gives us an opportunity to develop creative programs that expand students' imagination and supply an urgency to their study of history, literature, philosophy, and the arts."

> Service isn't merely a collection of one-time projects that build a resume—it's a way of life that can pervade all that we are and all that we do.

Lamb's vision is capacious. "My vocation is to teach as many competent citizens as possible," he says. And he will have help. In 2009, the John Templeton Foundation gave Wake Forest a grant of $3.7 million to launch a character project that supports Wake's own internal needs while also funding category-stretching research. Thanks to this and other philanthropic support, Wake Forest has been able to build a reservoir of in-house research on how character develops. Philosophy professor Christian Miller, author of *The Character Gap* and other books, is a nationally recognized authority on the subject. Wake professors Will Fleeson, Mike Furr, and Eranda Jayawickreme are making contributions from psychology. And the university's Eudaemonia Institute, dedicated to the interdisciplinary study of human flourishing, is run by business ethicist Jim Otteson, one of the world's leading authorities on the moral teachings of Adam Smith.

"Character includes a wide array of virtues," says Lamb. "It's more inclusive than we often think, and it's intrinsically related to the whole person.... Our relationships, our extending circles of love, are what make us whole."

The broader picture

Hatch admits that character education inevitably makes faculty nervous. "There are always blockages of, 'Who's going to define that?'" Many resist notions of moral hierarchies and preferred behavior, and don't want a conscious set of values promulgated in their classrooms. "The best way to kill an initiative is to birth it by requirements," Hatch says. "We'd rather try to do really good things and make them attractive."

One of the president's initiatives has been to make Wake Forest's admissions process interview-dependent. The aim is to attract people who have character and leadership gifts, not just academic credentials. Standardized tests are now optional, and the undergraduate application asks short-answer questions that try to get students to reflect on their priorities and direction. For instance:

• Hashtags trend worldwide. Give us a hashtag you wish were trending. Why?
• Describe yourself as fully and accurately as possible in the 140-character limit of a tweet.
• Choose an unsung historical figure who deserves the *Hamilton* musical treatment.
• Describe an instance in which you observed or exhibited "character."
• Give us your personal Top-10 list.

Wake has also invested heavily in student well-being, mentoring, and expanded faculty advising. Wake's THRIVE Initiative encourages practices of mindfulness and play. The Mentoring Resource Center invites public figures like Condoleeza Rice to discuss their life paths with students. It provides mentoring toolkits to departments at the university that want to connect their students to potential guides (like Andy Chan's office of personal and career development). They train individuals who want to be mentors to have deep conversations with students. They link younger students, older students, new graduates, alumni, and faculty in various small groups to encourage coaching, and affinity discussions.

For all the ways in which Wake has successfully adopted a renewed mission around character, it's still more of an aspiration than a proven path. The question that keeps Hatch up at night is a tough one: "How to do substantive character formation in a pluralistic context?" Some students and faculty are suspicious of Hatch's religious roots. Is he trying to impose his convictions? To make Wake a Christian institution?

"I can't impose my personal values on the university," Hatch says honestly. "But I can help shape it." He does feel that character development may be "impossible to do without religious resources," but he's also looking to recast these resources, and his institution's character-building efforts as a whole, in a distinctly pluralistic and forward-looking way.

"Wake Forest's religious heritage, far from being a liability or an embarrassment, offers the opportunity of a holistic education, one that allows students to wrestle with the world's most pressing issues," Hatch says. "We believe we can develop men and women of real character, people who do the right thing because it springs from their chosen commitments and values, not because it's legislated or imposed."

In his book *Education's End: Why Colleges and Universities Have Given Up on the Meaning of Life*, Anthony Kronman notes that he has "watched the question of life's meaning lose its status as a subject of organized academic instruction and seen it pushed to the margins of professional respectability in the humanities, where it once occupied a central and honored place."

Hatch and the colleagues he has gathered are restoring status to that question. From the curriculum's core requirements to the prime value placed on teaching, from the ways in which every Wake person you encounter—whether secretary, student, coach, or vice president—walks with a defined sense of belonging to the broader community, to the students' consistent aspiration to live lives defined by skilled competence in the service of civic care and contribution, no aspect of the Wake experience feels utilitarian or for show. Neither does any aspect seem detached from another. The school strives to integrate every strand into one message you can hang a life on, namely, that human beings are ends in themselves.

"I'd always thought of college as a financial tool to get a good job," says Sarah, who graduated with honors in 2017. "Never had I thought about the *why* of what I was doing. Until I came here."

Drew, a rising senior, says, "Here at Wake, you *know* people. You want to help the other out. It's always: 'How are you? And *who* are you?'"

"I think a lot of college presidents would like this," says Hatch. "But they don't know how to do it. Here at Wake Forest, we're driving a car. We as university leaders need to build the road."

Character Education at Scale
The Positivity Project
Raleigh, North Carolina

Great teachers...have not lifted human quality primarily by thundering against sin; they have lifted it by heightening the positive conception of life's dignity and value.
~ Harry Emerson Fosdick

I have a dream that my four little children will one day live in a nation where they will not be judged by the color of their skin, but by the content of their character.
~ Martin Luther King Jr.

Think of the last time you were in an environment where people truly knew one another, and felt known. Then imagine an entire middle school in a socioeconomically mixed urban neighborhood marked by this atmosphere of mutual understanding and intimacy, where you were known first by the content of your character. Such is the blooming reality at Carroll Magnet Middle School in Raleigh, North Carolina.

Five years ago, Carroll was chaotic. Students wandered the halls with no direction or zeal, seriously underperforming and getting into fights. Parents were yanking kids out in droves, and only those with no other choice—children from refugee families, the 50 percent who qualified for free and reduced lunch—were sticking around.

Then Elizabeth MacWilliams became principal in 2014. The driven, bounce-in-her-step go-getter began visiting homes, riding school buses, and inviting families to become involved with the school. She built trust, and an awareness that a new regime was in place at the middle school. "Beyond the instructional leadership and managerial responsibilities," says MacWilliams, "principals are charged with being hustlers, advocates, and mentors."

And the new leader did more than just inject energy. The most visible new element at Carroll Middle School is the emphasis on character-building. Encouragement of constructive behavior is enshrined on stairwells, classroom doors, and teacher nametags—and reflected in the daily manners of students.

These lessons and exhortations come from The Positivity Project, a program founded in 2015 by Mike Erwin. He is a retired military officer and trained expert in the field of positive psychology that was developed by Chris Peterson and Martin Seligman in the 1990s. Erwin's Positivity Project is an easy-to-use, cost-effective character-building tool now being tried in 494 schools around the country, Carroll being one.

It begins by establishing a shared vocabulary of moral sentiments. After studying all the major religions and philosophical traditions, then conducting many surveys and behavioral experiments, Peterson and Seligman distilled out six virtues that have been shared in practically all cultures across three millennia. Under each of these major virtues, the researchers further specified three to five "character strengths," of similarly proven value across time and place, that feed that outcome. Here are the six virtues, and related character strengths, as codified by The Positivity Project:

- Wisdom (perspective, love of learning, open-mindedness, curiosity, creativity)
- Courage (bravery, perseverance, integrity, enthusiasm)
- Humanity (love, kindness, social intelligence)
- Justice (fairness, teamwork, leadership)
- Temperance (self-control, prudence, humility, forgiveness)
- Transcendence (purpose, gratitude, optimism, humor, appreciation of beauty & excellence)

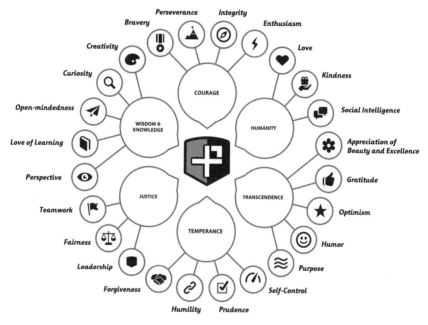

(Peterson and Seligman, 2004)

The 24 Character Strengths that Positivity Project schools invite each student, teacher, custodial staffer, and administrator to consider within themselves and in others.

Erwin had lots of firsthand experience as a leader. He was a high-level athlete, trained as a West Point cadet, deployed as an intelligence officer for special forces in Iraq and Afghanistan, and later founded of one of today's best new charities for veterans—Team Red,

White & Blue. When he attended graduate school at the University of Michigan and studied with Chris Peterson (whose favorite saying was "other people matter"), Erwin became fascinated with the six virtues and 24 strengths identified under positive psychology, and immersed himself in the field.

For Erwin, character is more than exemplary actions or individual achievement. "It's a broad and complex family of thoughts, feelings, and behaviors that are recognized and encouraged across cultures for the values they bring to people and society." The Positivity Project teaches that character is the aggregate of traits, carried around to different degrees inside each of us, that allow a society to prosper. No single trait should overwhelm the others; to flourish, people need to keep balance among the two dozen valuable qualities.

Erwin has created a set of tools that make it simple for principals and teachers to bring this knowledge into schools. Once a school's principal decides it will become "a Positivity Project school," everyone in the building—students, teachers, and all staff—takes a 15-minute test called the Values In Action Character Strengths Survey. The VIA survey was developed by Peterson and Seligman with funding from the Mayerson Family Foundation. It asks you to agree or disagree with statements like, "I never quit a task before it is done," "I like to think of new ways to do things," "I rarely hold a grudge," and "Even when candy or cookies are under my nose, I never overeat." There are separate versions for youth and for adults. After you've finished, you get a ranked list of your 24 character strengths.

It's genuinely fun, yet grounded in social science. "When I took the survey and it showed my top strengths, I was like, 'Wow, that's definitely me,' " says Victoria Cooke, an eighth-grader. "And when other students tell me their results, I often think, 'Yes, I see that.' "

Character training in action
At Carroll, time is spent during the first week of each new school year taking the test and discussing results in a way that encourages collective reflection. Students are asked, Who are you? What do you bring to the table? Why are we all here? After that school-wide launch, all students participate in a daily, full-year 30-minute class, where they learn how to develop personal strengths (and blunt weaknesses). Then they are encouraged to have discussions in their lunch group, which carries the lessons over to middle-school social life.

"What's hard for you to control?" asks Ms. Geter in a pre-lunch session with seventh graders. "Anger," says Josiah. "Anger and laughter," offers Adonis. "Irritability," answers Lauren. As the kids take turns admitting their struggles, the other kids steal glances at one another with nods and knowing chuckles, enjoying the act of recognizing a gift or flaw in their classmates.

"Irritability, that's a good one," says Geter, a corrections officer turned teacher. "Do we all know what it means to be irritable?" In this fashion, the Carroll students zero in on each of the 24 character strengths for two weeks each.

"Why is it important for us to have self-control?" Geter asks her classroom. "Well, without self-control the majority of the human race might be dead by now," replies Gretchen.

"True," responds the teacher with a chuckle. "When I was a corrections officer, that prison was filled with a whole lot of emotional people. And they'd just explode. They didn't think. They went from zero to one hundred."

The Positivity Project gives students new ways of understanding their emotions. And there seems to be little shame among them in acknowledging what they need to work on. Without some mechanism like this, "kids aren't able to really articulate what it is that's driving their discomfort or impulsivity," suggests MacWilliams. She believes the program gives troubled students in particular a language for making sense of frustrations.

At the end of her session, Geter asks the students why they are working on these traits. "Because other people matter!" the class shouts in unison. The kids clearly enjoy the process of growing in self-awareness.

A few years after becoming a Positivity Project school, Carroll middle school is almost unrecognizable. From a dwindling population of 600 students its headcount is now up to 1,003 and counting. MacWilliams has created new mentoring opportunities that allow students to spend time with local professionals. And while qualitative gains are being made in student character, quantitative academic gains have rocketed alongside, with a 35-point leap in the proficiency rate in math and double-digit spikes in other subjects.

Value and use

The Positivity Project can help students overcome divisions centered on things like race and class, putting the focus instead on a person's character. When Mike Erwin asked Carroll students during a recent tour of the school to talk about the gifts and challenges of their diversity as a student body, kids answered, "We're super diverse—my strengths are appreciation for beauty and excellence, humility, and spirituality. His top strengths are bravery, teamwork, and perseverance."

"At my old school," says eighth-grader Victoria Cooke, "we were all racially divided. You stayed in your spot. That's how I grew up. That's how most schools work. When I came to Carroll everyone was nice to each other. Before, most of my friends were black and I hadn't really dealt with different races. Now, I have whole types of different friends."

When I asked some Carroll students, "What do you find to be the most important aspect of a person?" they unanimously answered: "The personality."

"My old school was nothing like this," says sixth-grader Henry Foster. "Here people talk, relate. If you see someone with the same strengths you have, it comes out."

> The Positivity Project gives students new ways of understanding their emotions. And there seems to be little shame among them in acknowledging what they need to work on.

"At my old school the teachers and students were never in real relationships," says Henry. "One of my teachers had a kid, and because she didn't wear a ring, when I finally found out I was like, 'Huh? You have a kid?' It was just, 'I'm the teacher, you're the student. That's how it is.' There was no learning anything personal about each other."

A big question is, does deepening self-knowledge, and knowledge of others, actually lead to better education? To win over today's educators who have been trained to protect self-esteem and individual expression, and to avoid dwelling on students' weaknesses, The Positivity Project uses the language of "strength" rather than flaw. The strengths scorecard allows every student to be "exceptional."

But talking about personal strengths all the time doesn't necessarily mend personal weaknesses, which is one essential role of education. How much accountability and expectation of difficult self-reform is built into this process? "We're supposed to be not just focusing on our top five, but also on our bottom five," acknowledges MacWilliams. But she argues that "our greatest faults often link to our strengths," and "just knowing these things about ourselves can help us approach adversity or challenge."

One justification for The Positivity Project's heavy investment of time and classroom energy in emotional exploration is the expectation that this will then make other priorities—academic learning, social peace, etc.—more attainable. "My first year here," recalls MacWilliams, "fights would break out and kids would circle around and be interested, instead of trying to help. Now, I see kids really sticking up for each other, trying to protect one another."

MacWilliams acknowledges that Carroll Middle School hasn't solved all of its problems. But she's satisfied that "The Positivity Project has become part of the kids' language, part of their coping mechanism. It helps them think, 'Wait a minute, this is who I am, and I can always reach into that toolbox when I need it.'"

Positivity Project founder Mike Erwin thinks the program can be useful in thousands of schools. Already it is operating in 494 schools and touching 340,000 students. But his venture is still young, and small—a full-time staff of three, plus Erwin and his co-founder Jeff Bryan. And before they will put funds behind it, many philanthropists want more data on results than this four-year-old venture is so far capable of providing.

A couple of foundation representatives described to me why they took a chance on Erwin, and would encourage others to do the same. "Part of the appeal of The Positivity Project is Mike himself," explains Meg O'Connell of the Allyn Family Foundation in Syracuse, New York. Allyn invested $60,000 into general operations for the nonprofit over two years. "He has such a solid reputation as a motivational coach and leader, and what he's brought from his military experience to these concepts is impressive. He's done his homework, and can articulate a vision for how this program can change schools."

What attracted O'Connell, and the schools that have so far experimented with The Positivity Project, "was that it wasn't going to cost a lot of money to implement. Schools need the staff to commit, and they need to sign an agreement. But beyond that, it's quick." The "character-in-a-box" design of the project, with user-friendly curriculum modules and training for teachers, were designed specifically to make it easy to expand the program nationally.

The Heinz Endowments in Pittsburgh has also been a funder, putting up the money to bring the effort to eight schools in Pittsburgh.

"Too often, foundations like ours have evaluated school reform solely by looking at student achievement and academic performance, ignoring things like social-emotional learning," says Stanley Thompson of the Endowments. He says Heinz sees the value of programs that help students think of others before themselves, that help them become better citizens. "When you bring those things into the school, it can spill out into the larger community. That what was exciting to me about The Positivity Project."

The consulting firm McKinsey & Co heard about The Positivity Project and started talking with leaders at the partner schools about its formula. The firm assessed the organization's mission, vision and operations. McKinsey is sufficiently enthused that it's offering these contributions to The Positivity Project on a pro-bono basis.

McKinsey, Thompson, and O'Connell are anxious to see how wide a range of schools Erwin can succeed in. "The effort has been successful in our central New York region," O'Connell says, "but in more of the suburban school districts. I know he's also done well in North Carolina. I'd love to test it in some of our urban school districts where the need is greater. It's hard because the teachers are so busy, and the urban challenges so stiff."

"The challenge for Mike is to convince school leaders with data that when you start with the social-emotional learning needs of kids, then you're going to have successes in the academic realm which can't be won otherwise. He needs to persuade them that this is a foundational piece."

That's a crucial issue that must be addressed not only by this effort but by any character-building effort that demands school time. Nonetheless, The Positivity Project is betting on their own theory winning. It's up to donors to figure out how to assess the relational foundations such that these become the starting point for the academic success and whole-person development everyone wants to see.

Learning from the Past, Facing the Future
The Boy Scouts, USA

Where is there a boy to whom the call of the wild
and the open road does not appeal?
~ Robert Baden-Powell

A man's usefulness depends upon his living up to his ideals
insofar as he can. It is hard to fail but it is worse never to have tried
to succeed. All daring and courage, all iron endurance of misfortune make for a
finer, nobler type of manhood.
~ Theodore Roosevelt

Mention the phrase "character-forming institution" to an American male of a certain generation, and chances are high he will invoke the Boy Scouts. The most popular youth movement in American history, the Scouts became the preeminent virtue-building organization of the twentieth century, influencing a web of other civic institutions. More than 105 million boys have participated in the program, including disproportionate numbers of leaders. To this day, the Boy Scouts remain an icon of the sort of citizen that once made America exceptional and proud.

But times have changed, for better and for worse. As this is written, the Boy Scouts of America is considering filing for bankruptcy. The organization has been tossed about by cultural waves, the most recent relating to changing norms around gender and sexuality. The brand carries baggage. Functionally, Scouting has been damaged by declines in volunteering and community activity, the shifting structure of modern families, conflicting messages around basic notions of masculinity, and pervasive cultural swells toward self-advancement, away from character and community.

So this historic organization finds itself in a moment of transition: Can it find some fresh pathways to providing the moral clarity, civic pride, and shared ethos that its millions of alumni cherish? As philanthropists consider the context for character in our time, what lessons can the successes and struggles of BSA teach that might help us create new institutions?

Some history

Contrary to popular belief, the Boy Scouts were founded not as an organic outgrowth of traditional mores, but as a deliberate response to a society in the throes of deep change. Industrialization had drawn a massive influx of rural people to the cities, immigrants were flocking in unprecedented numbers, and the hardscrabble, patriotic ethos that had governed the tail end of the nineteenth century seemed to be unraveling. Boys once raised on farms were now reared in alleyways, conventional forms of religion had become unfashionable, and older generations looked askance at the rising generation of "flat-chested" men, defined more by idle gratuity than "usefulness."

There was William James's famous speech at Stanford University in 1906, "The Moral Equivalent of War," in which he questioned whether there could be any substitute for war in uniting the country and inculcating civic virtue. In 1910, the *New York Times* published an editorial entitled

"Making Good Soldiers Out of Schoolboys," which suggested that a youth movement might be needed to maintain national unity and global strength. "Our martial spirit is gone," lamented General William Verbeck in March of 1911. "What can we expect from our female school teachers? They have no military spirit. Our suffragettes have no military spirit. Our socialists have no military spirit.... We have the germ of a military spirit in Wall Street. There is grit there. In some of our business circles we have the spirit, 'Don't tread on me.' That is the military spirit. That we must develop." With a world war careening around the bend, it was a time of anxiousness about national purpose, male spine, and the nature of American greatness.

Meanwhile, over in the United Kingdom, a man named Robert Baden-Powell was testing answers to the question: "How do you make citizens and manufacture moral fiber?" Britain was in a crisis mood around the turn of the century. Its global economic and military dominance was collapsing, and its spiritual strength was all but gone. Baden-Powell wanted to create an efficient source of recruits for the defense of empire, a "character factory" whose human products might remedy Britain's moral, physical, and military weakness. He wanted to resurrect the "stout yeomen of yesteryear."

He found that a manual he had written while in South Africa to train soldiers in military reconnaissance, called *Aids to Scouting*, had been adopted by boys and youth groups looking for outdoor adventures, and even educators like Charlotte Mason (guiding spirit behind The Oaks Academy), becoming a surprise bestseller. Baden-Powell scanned the bloom of Boys' Brigades, Woodcraft Indians, Epworth Leagues, Sunday Schools, and YMCAs popping up across Britain and America and realized there was a hunger for groups that would test, discipline, and stretch young men. He rewrote his military manual for early adolescents and published it as *Scouting for Boys* in 1908. It took off, soon institutionalizing into the Scouts.

From the beginning, Baden-Powell's Scouts depended upon a coherent ideology. "Stressing unquestioning obedience to properly structured authority, happy acceptance of one's social and economic position in life, and an unwavering, uncritical patriotism, for which one would be willing, if necessary, to die, he saw the Scouts as the key both to social utility and personal fulfillment," wrote Michael Rosenthal in his 1984 history *The Character Factory*.

As legend has it, in 1909 an American philanthropist named William Boyce found himself lost on a foggy street in London. An unknown

Scout came to his aid, guiding him to his destination. When the Scout refused his offer of a tip and Boyce asked why, the boy explaining that he was a Boy Scout and was merely doing his daily good turn. Boyce was intrigued, consulted with Baden-Powell, and took his inspiration across the Atlantic, establishing the Boy Scouts of America in 1910.

From seeds to success: The genius of a movement

The Scouts took off in the States, quickly and unreservedly. Newspapers were almost breathless with excitement: "We hail the new age of chivalry which Young America ushers in," trumpeted a *New York Times* editorial in 1910. "The work takes in the entire range of moral and physical development perhaps as no other system yet devised has done. It gives something for every kind of boy."

In the early years, it was all about recovering the beau ideal of the daring man. Combining "ancient knowledge of nature" with modern knowledge and organization, the movement claimed to "put back some of the wild man into the city boys." Thrift was the "grit" of its day. Chivalry would be taught alongside opportunities for courage and self-sacrifice. There would be a chance for iron to sharpen iron, for wildness to be checked by civility, for bravery to be checked by chivalry.

Key to achieving this sort of balanced citizenship was the Scout merit system, which gave boys a clear pathway to prove themselves and advance in rank. The belief was that everyone could become great in character, resourcefulness, and self-reliance. Boys just needed a structure, a team, and a different kind of education, one that would be highly physical—man versus wild.

"We don't say, 'Come and be good boys,'" Baden-Powell told the *New York Times* during a North American visit in 1910. "That has wrecked other movements. We say: 'Come and be Indians,' and this appeals to their undeveloped minds. After attracting them we teach them until they come to know the value of handicraft. They pass into useful work, such as forming fire brigades, life-saving corps, and other useful branches that go to the making of good government."

Part of the genius of Scouting was its sheer appeal to boys. "Adventure!" reads the opening sentence of the longtime *Boy Scout Handbook*. "That's what Scouting is. You are standing at the door-way to the most exciting adventures you can imagine." Action was everything. Boy Scouts were given tools—outside the family context—to save another's life, to survive in the woods, to solve problems with others, and to rise to leadership when the occasion called. "At age 11 and 12," notes Chris Trepky, a modern-day Eagle Scout who is now 32, "you exist in a world where you don't have a lot of agency. The Scouts grant agency. It's a safe place for young men to fail."

Even today's *Boy Scout Handbook* reveals an education process that is less about schooling and more about facing a sequence of challenges in order to rise to a set of natural conclusions. It's an education in practical wisdom, with frequent opportunities to lead, not just follow a teacher. There are lessons in outdoor adventures, in what it means to grow from a boy to a man, in one's responsibilities as a Scout and as an American, and clear demands on the path to Eagle rank, the highest honor.

"Scouting gives you a chance to experience the world in a more real and meaningful way," says Trepky, "because otherwise you're living a life where everyone is telling you how things work. When you're in the BSA, you get to go find out for yourself. They're all about kindling a fire, not filling a vessel."

"At school," Trepky says, he got to "go on field trips and stuff like that. But I got to *do* stuff with the Boy Scouts. I got to learn more at my own pace. It was very self-directed, especially as I got older. It was a completely different delivery method than I got in public school. The BSA creates an environment where you can pursue your own goals. Men learn to find self-motivation."

The extraordinary levels of trust granted at an early age, combined with clear training in practical know-how, give Scouts a level-headedness that can define their moral responses throughout life. The Scouting ethic also imbues habits of mind that are acutely tuned to others, often instilling a sense of moral responsibility to help one's fellow citizens that lasts a lifetime.

"Rank advancement and the merit badges provided a codified system for proving competence," says Trepky. "We trusted in it, and as a result we were able to extend that trust into real life activities. The Boy Scouts gave me both the ability and the confidence to save someone's life. And that's powerful. Learning first aid...I realized I had the tools to be able to preserve someone's life on earth. I started to see myself as someone who could do that and would do that, given the opportunity."

The Scouts' other great insight has always been to keep power at the local level. To this day, local chartering organizations set their own standards with BSA troops. "A Boy Scout troop is only as sorted as the community that it comes from," says Trepky. "Most decisions get made at the unit level. And while troops may look very different from each other, the ethos is the same."

Scouts are visible, Trepky says, "and we lead the way in community service. I would not be surprised if the mayor of my town called the scoutmaster in times of crisis. That's certainly the first person I'd get to know if I were mayor, because the Scouts are a reserve I can tap any time, day or night."

Proud as it was of its distinctive mission, the BSA from its very beginning chose cooperation over territoriality. The organization's first public meeting was held in the auditorium of the YMCA, and Jacob Riis, photographer of *How the Other Half Lives*, keynoted. The Boy Scouts joined Jane Addams's Settlement House movement to celebrate the birthday of George Washington. In 1913, the LDS Church started using the Boy Scouts as its youth group for boys. Leaders of other youth movements were enlisted to spread the word on its offerings, along with public figures like former President Theodore Roosevelt.

The Scout education process is less about schooling and more about facing a sequence of challenges. It's an education in practical wisdom, with frequent opportunities to lead.

Its partnerships and openness helped the BSA grow quickly. The group soon became a key thread of the institutional re-weave that was going on socially and morally in America. People came to trust those associated with the Boy Scouts. Its brand was one of reliability, good citizenship, and high leadership. It was an everyman's movement for building America's mushrooming middle class. And it flourished as such for nearly a century.

Character fruits
In positions of leadership today, whether in the military, politics, business, philanthropy, or elsewhere, there is an inordinate amount of Boy Scout experience. Of America's first 312 astronauts, 180 were scouts, including 11 of the 12 men who walked on the moon. Other Scout alums include President Gerald Ford, novelist Wallace Stegner, businessmen and

philanthropists Sam Walton, Stephen Bechtel, and David Weekley, and many others. It's impressive. But more impressive is the ethos that Scouting imparted that to this day guides millions of American men, making a quiet difference on a daily basis in communities and organizations across our land.

In 2012 the John Templeton Foundation funded a Baylor University study of Eagle Scouts. The results were notable. The study found that throughout their adult lives those who had attained the rank of Eagle Scout tended to show a significantly greater connectedness to siblings, neighbors, religious community, friends, and coworkers. They were more active in formal and informal groups. They felt a spiritual presence in nature and acknowledged higher duties to God. These former Eagles participated in health and recreational activities at elevated rates, and were protective of the natural environment. They were more likely to be involved in community service, and in leadership positions. They were above average in planning and preparedness, and more likely than others to practice professional ethics, morality, tolerance, and respect for diversity.

"If I see that there's a medical emergency in front of me," reports Trepky, "I personally feel that I have a moral obligation to help, because I know how…. If you're walking in circles on the street and you look like you're not there, you look like you're having a hard time, I'm going to ask you what's happening. I'm at least going to reach out to you: 'Hey, you all right?' I want to see your eyes, I want to see if you're there. If I think you're not, I'm going to follow you for a second and I'm going to try to see, are you with it? Are you okay? I'm interested in that. Because I don't want you walking around on the street and getting hit, endangering somebody else or yourself. This is my city, this is where I live, I'm responsible for this."

Historically, many communities have relied upon the renaissance bag of skills that the BSA cultivates. It's still relatively easy for a troop to find sponsorship in a given community, especially in small towns or suburbs, in part because many of the local business owners will have Scout badges of their own.

"When I was starting my Eagle project," recalls Trepky, "I needed some lumber, and I walked in a lumber yard and said, 'Hi, I'm a Boy Scout and I'm trying to do a project, and I'm looking for somebody that I can talk to.' A ten-minute conversation later the guy was like, 'Well, what do you need?' And I gave him a list…. He said, 'You look very organized, I'd be happy to get you this stuff. You can have it free of charge, don't worry about it.'"

Others describe the Boy Scouts as providing a coming-of-age pathway when other routes weren't open. David Weekley co-founded the country's largest private homebuilding company and is a respected philanthropist based in Houston. He has been involved in Scouts since he was a kid, most recently serving on some of the organization's highest boards.

"I was a little chubby, fat kid, never the smartest or best-looking," Weekley recalls. "But for me, I could go in and I could work hard and get badges, and be somebody. The Boy Scouts were a place where you could work and get affirmation, work and take responsibility, because somebody outside your family was paying attention and pushing you." Stan Swim of the Bill of Rights Institute is a longtime Scout who later became a Scoutmaster in Salt Lake City. He understands the Scouts as providing a place for boys to confront real challenges in a culture that wants to rip that experience away.

"Our group helps boys learn to accomplish genuinely difficult things. In an urban or even suburban environment, it often seems like the most challenging things boys do are in the context of athletics. And that's fine; there's some real value for athletics in character formation, especially when it comes to teams. But they don't teach you how to solve problems in solitude, particularly when the impediments are your own limitations, which you need to break through on your own. And there's a lot of praise and adulation that accompanies the athletic experience today. That seems to dilute its value and cause the boys to become too transactional and superficial in the pursuit of achievement. In Scouts, there's nobody to dish out attaboys."

The BSA also provides a needed counterweight to technological distractions. "Are we raising a generation of young men who will be led to believe that their life is complete with what you can learn from a screen?" asks Swim. "That would be a tremendous tragedy. It would bode poorly for that person, and also for the society. Scouts does not allow you to treat the outdoors as some tourist destination where you go out and take a few pretty pictures. Rather, it's 'How do you grapple with nature on its own? Where do you fit in that whole process? How do you go through a survival experience?'"

He also sees the Scouts as one of the last organizations to be teaching American history properly. "We don't have a good replacement for passing along our American heritage now. I don't think the public schools are on the case there. I think they have deliberately quit that field. With all this nation's imperfections, its story is still an essential part of what kids need to know. And it's not being taught outside the Scouts."

Challenges today

Despite these many successes, the Boy Scouts have encountered serious challenges in recent years. This is reflected in enrollment decline. Today, 2.3 million boys are involved in Scouting. The historic peak was around 4 million.

BSA's struggles to navigate deep shifts in American society are the same ones that confront many other efforts to promote robust character formation today. There is the pressure to choose between tradition and pluralism. There are changing notions of gender, now at a fundamental level. There is a privatization and specialization of leisure and recreational activity. Family time pressures and the pressures of performance have squeezed the average childhood of simple play and fun, relationship building, and renaissance breadth. There are general declines in volunteerism, and a loss of available fathers to help lead troops. There is the erosion of the middle class, historically the bastion of Scouting. With changing U.S. demography there is a need to attract minority troop leaders and better serve minority youth.

Board members of BSA are aware of these challenges, and are trying hard to address them. "The Boy Scouts started at a moment in history that was very community-based," Weekley points out. "People lived in the same place for a long time. They knew their neighbors. Parents have less time today." The rise of homes with two working parents means there is less connection. For single moms, there's almost no ability to drop off a kid, let alone volunteer.

"In my small Midwestern town," reflects Trepky, "if your parents weren't available to drop you off on a Friday and pick you up on a Sunday, someone else in the town would volunteer to do it. We took care of one another. But I'm not sure that's true in most places today. It's a big lift for a single parent."

"I think the whole volunteerism culture has changed," says Weekley. "The amount of time that people have has changed. The competitiveness of society has changed."

On the other side of the coin, the rise of the helicopter parent has also hurt the BSA. The organization preaches hardiness, making mistakes on your own and responding with mental toughness and thrift. Parents may say they want their kids to be gritty, but as soon as they hear what the troop is serving for breakfast, they go nuts. "Mom will come up to the troop leader and say, 'Well, Jimmy's got to have his protein bar in the morning,'" Weekley sighs. "So we now have a parental obstacle to building the self-reliance that's always been our hallmark."

Parental coddling frustrates many BSA goals. "There are more folks worried about triggering unhappiness, and anxious to encourage self-expression today," says Weekley. "Our therapeutic culture seems to block the normal Scout, tough-love way of doing things. Moms are ripping their kids out of troops that they find too disciplined, even if the troop is just emphasizing fundamental character traits."

There is a loss of generational links. Trepky's dad helped lead his troop. "I loved the Scouts because I watched my dad do it. I wanted to be just like him." The Weekley family was also part of that common experience. "For a long time, guys like me who loved the Scouts, were shaped by the Scouts, we would just send our sons and keep enrollment levels steady," says Weekley.

> The rise of the helicopter parent has also hurt the Scouts. The organization preaches hardiness, making mistakes on your own, and responding with mental toughness and grit.

But demographic changes are leaving fewer longtime fans to feed the rolls. And BSA's cultural expansion hasn't kept pace. Current predictions see 2050 as the year when the U.S. becomes a majority nonwhite nation. The Scouts are not naïve to this, and have tried to reach out to various ethnic communities with sensitivity and an eagerness to stretch their style of delivery to woo new boys.

But the results have been modest. "It's not that we haven't tried," says Weekley. "We've spent time and money, we've been working with Latino leaders, we've started specifically Latino initiatives, we hired the best Latino marketing guys in the country to help us. We've now got Spanish speakers involved in almost every region, but there just doesn't seem to be a culture of sending boys off on independent, organized adventures."

And if today's parents didn't do it themselves, or aren't familiar with it, they're a lot harder to persuade; it sounds like just one more thing they have to do for their kids. "Scouting has succeeded historically in part because we had plenty of available and willing volunteers," says Weekley. "We've somehow not been able to make the Scouts visible to the institutional volunteering of a black or Hispanic community."

And then there's the culture war. The last decade saw a highly publicized outcry over the BSA's refusal to allow gay Scout leaders. In 2015, BSA shifted and began allowing local troops to accept gay adult leaders, and, more recently, girls and transgender boys. The first decision sparked some exodus, but the latest moves have caused a real furor, especially because the decisions were made at the national level of the organization, seemingly disempowering local troops. The organization also changed its name to Scouts BSA. The Mormon church, Scouting's largest faith-based partner, accounting for nearly 20 percent of Boy Scouts, announced it would sever its ties with BSA. Evangelical families also started exiting, forming their own similar organization called Trail Life USA, which now has 30,000 members.

"I fear the most recent decisions may accelerate declining membership," says Weekley. "As the Scouts were continuing to stay strong in what their belief system was, they kept losing members. And so then they capitulated and now I'm afraid they're going to lose more members because their core feels disenfranchised."

Trepky, a millennial, hopes the engrained localism of Boy Scout management will allow the group to weather this storm.

"Everything in the BSA happens at the troop level," he says, "including the trans thing, including the leadership thing. BSA made it clear when it released the new rules that this was a decision that would be made at the troop level and negotiated with your chartering organization—which many times is a church."

He argues that "BSA has never been about the national organization. It's always been about the troop. There's a respect for 'you do you'—a genuine localism. The BSA doesn't believe it should dictate what's best for a particular community. It doesn't have that hubris. That's how it's stayed relevant all these years. If it had these edicts coming down from up high, it'd be just as divided as the rest of the country, and we wouldn't be efficient at doing anything."

Swim is less optimistic. "There are things that boys need Scouting to uniquely do for them. What worries me, as we enter what I call the age of uniformity, is that we don't like to tolerate the idea that an organization would not like to serve everybody. As any parent can tell you, there's an enormous difference between your son and your daughter. The pendulum has swung too far toward uniformity, in the noble name of equality. We have a punishing cultural attitude now that says, 'If you can't do it for everyone, there must be something wrong with it.' That concerns me."

"I don't think the BSA is irreplaceable," warns Swim. "I think that leaders of any organization that do this kind of reactive stuff lose their organization. You only matter if you are really serving the boys that you set out to serve. I feel really bad when these national issues get distracting, and when the focus starts to be about things other than the boys."

Trepky remains hopeful. "I think the Boy Scouts will be around for as long as the United States," he says. It's an interesting comment, one which may actually put more onus on the country than the Scouts. Will divisive social issues squeeze the Scouts' effectiveness and allure? Is the current discouragement simply a product of an older generation lamenting changing times? Or has society changed so fundamentally that the BSA formula has lost its magic? That remains to be seen.

One thing, though, is clear: Losing an organization that has proven it can chisel young men in the ways of virtue and responsibility, self-sacrifice and teamwork, by offering them personal demands and brotherhood and the irreplaceable challenges of the outdoors, so that they can believe in something beyond their tribe and beyond themselves—this would be a civic loss.

"There's a lot of places you can get a good character, cultural, religious, civic education," says Trepky. "But there are very few places where you can get them all at once. The Boy Scouts are a social environment all its own." In a nation that needs citizens who carry a sense of cooperative responsibility and individual competence, we should wish for more such places, not fewer.

EXPLAINING THE PARADIGM:
16 Questions for Givers and Institutional Leaders

Now that you have read these narratives, let's revisit the 16 features I described at the outset. These are those traits I've observed to be present in the most effective character-forming institutions today, features that really should be present in any healthy organization, character-focused or not. They are the 16 features which, when working well, form people and prepare them to enter the most meaningful covenants of life: vocation, family, community, and faith. Most importantly, it is in these kinds of communities that people grasp their own moral agency.

What follows are the 16 Questions fleshed out. These may take varying forms in different kinds of organizations—closed versus open, nonprofit versus corporate, educational versus artistic, bureaucratic versus entrepreneurial. But hopefully they'll begin to get you thinking more capaciously about the conditions required for character to bloom. Conditions that you as a donor or institutional leader might be able to influence.

1. TELOS

Does the organization have a clear, strong reason for being in the world, embraced and pursued by all of its members? Does it give its members organizing criteria for what to love?

If you have a why to live for, you can withstand any how.
~ Friedrich Nietzsche

If there's one thing that marks today's erosion of institutions in civil society, it's a loss of what the Greeks called telos. Aristotle conceived of telos as that *why* and *to what end* one is living and laboring—a purpose beyond self. As many traditionally formative institutions have struggled to relate to an increasingly individualistic, consumerist, and utilitarian culture—be they churches, universities, voluntary service associations, or something as intimate as marriage—they have tended to lose sight of a transcendent mission as they've scrambled to meet the goals of their individual members. In the process, they often wind up losing both goods.

Ideally, a strong sense of telos unites people and raises them up out of themselves. It orients their energies and yokes their actions to their beliefs, often in the company of others. The most effective mission statements imply something normative, and they allow for a common frame of reference that creates a standard to abide by, leading naturally to a structure of accountability, a sense of responsibility, and an enduring moral identity. A strong institutional telos joins individuals to an arc beyond themselves. That sense of belonging leads people from small conversations about safety and comfort to large conversations, such as our relatedness and responsibility to one another and to a larger cause or community. A strong telos protects against selfishness, cynicism, and distrust. It allows for genuine, robust inquiry and free individual action. It lends meaning to struggle and pain, fostering individual grit and interdependence.

Take the U.S. military. Its mission places the individual in existential service to the country at large. With the stated end being to protect the U.S. and to fight and win the country's wars, a list of core values naturally follows: loyalty, duty, respect, selfless service, honor, integrity, and personal courage. The military's compelling purpose attracts people from vastly different backgrounds, chiseling one another and learning how to work together in the process.

Religious universities are another example. A school like Yeshiva, Notre Dame, or Brigham Young University has the advantage of locating itself in a larger tradition centered on deeper truths. Insofar as universities were founded to protect and facilitate a shared quest for truth, today's more rigorous religious colleges actually have a head start compared to their secular counterparts, which have come to understand learning merely as a means to one's career, nothing more uniting or inspiring. Wheaton College, for instance, exists "to integrate faith and learning" in the service "for Christ and His Kingdom."

A strong telos doesn't need to be as exclusive in its beliefs as Wheaton's is, but it does need to be sufficiently specific in its implications that all of the institution's activity, culture, and logic are informed by a clear direction. Universities that have maintained their original motto and consistently measure all activities and changes against it tend to maintain their capacity to form—even amidst today's distractions and moral cacophony.

The Latin motto of the University of Chicago is *Crescat scientia; vita excolatur.* "Let knowledge grow from more to more; and so be human life enriched." The school took an independent stand in 2016 against "safe spaces" and "trigger warnings" in a letter to its incoming freshman class. This letter, followed by a matriculation speech from law professor Geoffrey Stone, explained clearly the reason for protecting the free exchange of ideas. "Academic freedom is, in fact, a hard-bought acquisition in an endless struggle to preserve the right of each individual, student and faculty alike, to seek wisdom, knowledge, and truth, free of the censor's sword," said Stone to the freshmen. A university's role is to "instill in its students and faculty the importance of winning the day by facts, by ideas and by persuasion, rather than by force, obstruction, or censorship." He knew what the University of Chicago was about— seeking truth as a community of learners—and thus had ground to stand athwart prevailing collegiate winds.

Every strong telos of a character-building institution should have an expression in a mission statement, but not every mission statement implies a strong telos. Some missions are deeper or more focused than others. The key is to see if the statement answers three tests: (1) Is it in service of something beyond the individual member's own development? (2) Does the mission statement have a clear moral purpose embedded within it? (3) Is it rooted in an identifiable tradition, even as it strains toward the unpredictable demands of the future?

2. LITURGIES & RITUALS
Is there a covenant or creed that is affirmed regularly as a community, in word and deed? Are there communal rhythms, routines, and rituals?

Liturgies aim our love to different ends precisely by training
our hearts through our bodies.... Liturgies make us certain kinds
of people, and what defines us is what we love.
~ James K. A. Smith

As human beings we're a strange blend of individual agency and interdependence. As unique as each of us is, we are also built to mimic others, from birth to adulthood. We find meaning by locating our lives within a broader context, which in turn grants direction and purpose.

But we live now in an age that glorifies the unfettered rights of the individual, his or her moral responsibility defined only by temporal group identity, not a transcendent moral creed. We balk at the idea of deferring to a set of rituals or committing to an organizational routine. We fear giving away our own power, and assume that freedom of conscience means standing apart from institutional overhead, from hierarchy, from a set of absolute proclamations about what is good or true.

Considered reaction against empty forms and abuses of power is commendable. But today's trust in the individual's capacity to find his or her own flourishing is extreme. An older wisdom says that real liberty involves paradox: Tie yourself down to the right things, and you will find true freedom. Commit to a set of repeated rhythms in the company of others, and gradually, if mysteriously, a deeper personality will bloom.

There are a variety of longstanding institutions that stake their success on this theory. Liturgies and rituals are of course the basic ingredients of all the historic religions, with regular recitations of creeds, cycles of fasting and feasting, liturgical calendars and concentric circles of sacred daily, weekly, monthly practices.

The military is another example. From the morning bugle to evening taps, salutes to covering each dead soldier's casket with a flag, rituals speak to the institution's ultimate telos: to serve and sacrifice for one's country. Even when informal, "off-the-book" rituals get established—fighter pilots getting hosed down after their final flight, Marine infantrymen shaving their heads for their first deployment—the point is the same: Develop a set of traditions, and you will find yourself not only further bonded to your comrades, but the conscious heir of a heroic lineage.

Williamson College of the Trades is a vocational and character-building training school in Pennsylvania that relies upon a carefully structured environment of daily chapel, work details, a dress code, and clearly defined rules and responsibilities. The goal is to produce "The Williamson Man" in each graduate, known throughout their future careers as crewmen of integrity and humble leadership.

Five out of the six narrative features in this very book rely on a set of rituals to orient the community and grant it an identity and purpose. The Scouts from their founding have revolved around an oath, a law, a motto, a slogan, and an outdoor code, all of which are recited aloud and reflected upon at various junctures. The Oaks Academy begins each day with songs in the foyer, the parents standing side by side with their children. The Other Side Academy is defined by ritual and monument. From the confessional "Games" to the matriculation and expulsion Bench to the 12 Beliefs that line every wall to the opening and closing ceremonies, everything is anchored in set scripts, their truths revealed over time and through personal discovery. The Positivity Project schedules a 30-minute slot every day before the lunch hour for groups of students to dissect their character strengths.

The point is, liturgies and rituals form us, and when they're taken seriously and followed by both leaders and members, they are also a sign that an institution wields a well-earned authority, that its leadership is trusted, that its members are humble and teachable, and that the institution at large believes in something beyond itself—something deep enough, and existential enough, to create ritual, and to sustain its practice. Rituals root us, remind us of who we are and why we are here, and also give us the resources from which to innovate and live authentically in a world of uncertainty.

An older wisdom says that real liberty involves paradox: Tie yourself down to the right things, and you will find true freedom.

3. FULL ENGAGEMENT by ALL MEMBERS
Are all members of the organization, regardless of position or stature, engaged in the mission and aware of the significance and contribution of their roles?

To belong to a community is to act as a creator and co-owner of that community. What I consider mine I will build and nurture. [Our task today] is to seek in our communities a wider and deeper sense of emotional ownership; it means fostering among all of a community's citizens a sense of ownership and accountability.
~ Peter Block, Community: The Structure of Belonging

Steven Reinemund, former CEO of PepsiCo, once observed that "the organizations with the best cultures encourage full engagement up and down the company hierarchy." He was talking about for-profit behemoths like Southwest Airlines, Chick-fil-A, and Zappos, but the same principle applies to nonprofit organizations in the character-forming business.

Organizations that engage every member of their staff in their mission, and win their full-throated investment, tend to foster a widespread sense of ownership and accountability.

As everyone participates willingly, even joyfully, a mutually enriching culture emerges—one that's intriguing to outsiders, that is trusting and transparent, that encourages personal responsibility, and that forms people's ethos in a consistent, recognizable way.

Take Wake Forest, for instance. Every person you talk to, whether it's a janitor, professor, student, or administrator, emanates a sense of pride in the institution he or she is serving. Wake's identity is rooted in an ethos of service and personalism, how you treat others is the mark of the well-formed man or woman. The school is small enough that each individual has the chance to know and be known, large enough that each can be challenged to stretch and mature. President Nathan Hatch comports himself in a way that matches his belief in the innate dignity of each person, and he has hired people of similar conviction. Employees at all levels and across Wake's undergraduate and graduate education, as well as its schools of business, divinity, law, and medicine, affirm their commitment to Wake's mission of developing the whole person, ensuring that knowledge, experience, and service are consistently reinforcing one another as the training pathway to a meaningful, responsible life.

Community Renewal also inspires this kind of all-in commitment and personal transformation. One person after another, whether rich or poor, white or black, has found a deeper fulfillment and purpose in renewing Shreveport's social fabric, and in turn being renewed. No one is left out. All relationships find need of restoration and growth, which leads to people very much unlike each other, and in this case with deep historic rifts, leaning in to the discomfort and finding themselves changed by the encounter.

The Other Side Academy in Salt Lake City, while "tough love" in its approach, speaks in a language of mutual service. Co-founder Joseph Grenny only feels gratitude for how he's being transformed, even as he watches these men and women find hope and a fresh life. Each person is invested in the success of the therapeutic community by sweat and by pledge, and to lose one is to experience a tear in the system helping to redeem your mistakes and transform your character.

Summer camp invites this all-in sense of belonging, as does a well-functioning family. The Twelve Step theory of addiction recovery is powerful in part because it's a level playing field: Everyone comes as an addict, and everyone pursues the same sequence of confession, surrender, discipline, and recovery—even if the process looks different for each person.

The key is for a leader to act like every person matters and has a unique contribution to make. Does he or she treat the weakest and the lowest with the same dignity as those at the top? This example, in cooperation with a strong mission or telos, should inspire the all-in participation that changes human beings. This will get trickier as the workforce becomes less traditional and the broader culture continues to encourage a scatterplot of ever-shifting commitments, but those institutions that are able to compel full investment, ownership, and accountability will be those that leave the deepest mark.

4. POWER of the PARTICULAR
Does the organization have a particular identity, a thick set of norms that gets passed on to its members? Does it have a unique quality that is recognizable in those it has shaped?

Don't try to be everyman. Don't pretend you're a member
of every community you visit. Don't try to be citizens of some artificial
globalized community. Go deeper into your own tradition. Call upon the
geography of your own past. Be distinct and credible. People will come.
~ David Brooks

All families have their own way of doing things. Quirks. Traditions spoken and unspoken, norms that have developed through habit and choice that build a particular legacy.

College fraternities and sororities have something similar. So does the military. As do many summer camps, geographic regions, religious communities, and some companies. When fellow campers see each other again, they speak in a certain dialect—often reverting back to acronyms, phrases, and camp identities the way adults revert back to childhood patterns when visiting parents for the holiday.

The institutions that have this tend to be "thick" organizations—thick with history and custom, webs of relationships, and a cherished story that they tell and retell. Thick organizations leave an imprint. Meet a Davidson College alum, for instance, and he or she will likely be intellectually curious, broadminded, committed to several civic efforts in his or her community, and repelled by moral shortcuts (such as cheating). Meet a graduate of Kenyon College, and he or she will be comfortable amid diverse viewpoints and able to navigate conflict with grace. Meet a West Pointer, and you can expect to see fortitude, humility, leadership skills, and a grounded wisdom. Many Eagle Scouts anchor a core part of their identity in being an Eagle Scout—for life. It's as much a private code as a public reputation.

By contrast, graduates of most big state schools are not as identifiable. They tend to find their most formative influence in a smaller sub-experience of the college, such as their sorority or their sports team. This gets to a related principle: The smaller the size of a given community, the more likely it is to be thick with customs, stories, motivation, and accountability. It's probably no accident that the Scouts, the military, many liberal arts classrooms, and business-school trainings structure their fundamental unit of action to hold between four and 20 participants.

But what does an institution's level of particularity have to do with character? It's not guaranteed that a distinct organization forms people in a good direction, merely that it forms them. But particularity is a clue, especially in a time tempted toward political correctness and being all things to all people, that an institution has a strong sense of self. It does not apologize for its customs, nor does it dilute its convictions. There's something sticky about it that makes you want to belong. Its sharpness of definition compels meaningful commitment.

Outward Bound has a way of honing its young people to take risks and be more rugged, to respect nature's force and learn survival skills with others. Most people who have gone through an Outward Bound experience have at once a flexible nature and a dependability, a quiet charisma and a problem-solving appetite. Cometa in Italy, through its emphasis on beauty and generosity without limit, has graduated a cascade of young people who now serve others through social entrepreneurship ventures that are as beautiful as they are practical, humane as they are committed to standards of excellence. Employers say, "Cometa students are different."

> Thick organizations tell and retell a cherished origin story, often incorporating the arts, especially songs, into daily life.

Thick institutions transcend our instrumental motivations—to get a degree or to earn a salary—to become instead part of our identities. The healthy ones tend to engage the whole person—head, hands, heart, and soul—in person, not online. They often have collective rituals, reciting or standing in formation or coming together at a frequent assembly. They have shared tasks, which often involve members closely watching one another. Thick organizations also tell and retell a cherished origin story about themselves, or about the larger tradition that animates them. Many incorporate the arts, especially songs, into daily life, and have a common ideal expressed in mottos and liturgies.

Traditionally, there have been particular professional codes, instilled through education, heritage, and an overt embrace of a moral ethos. "I'm not going to cheat because I'm a Davidson graduate," for instance. Or,

"I'm not going to drink to excess because I'm a doctor." Ideals were integrated into identity.

Law, for instance, was a profession that thought of itself as stewarding a long tradition of justice, a tradition indispensable to preserving a sense of social unity. It relied on principles like confidentiality, respect for the rules, and avoidance of false statements or conflicts of interest. In the last 30 years, however, the profession has changed, emphasizing the short-range concerns and rights of clients over and above the stewardship of a longstanding moral tradition. The profession's code has been diluted, either by a failure of transmission in the law schools or in the day-to-day practice of modern law. Lawyers no longer are required to pledge an oath to a set of standards beyond ethical technicalities that look more like compliance and job preservation than a deep moral affirmation.

5. WHOLE PERSON
Does the organization have a clear conception of the whole person—head, heart, and helping hand—and seek to develop it? Are employees and departments integrated across domains, serving constituents in complementary, mutually reinforcing ways?

> *Education is a holistic endeavor that involves the whole person, including our bodies, in a process of formation that aims our desires, primes our imagination, and orients us to the world—all before we ever start "thinking" about it.*
> **~ James K. A. Smith**

Character is a whole-person phenomenon. It does not get transmitted merely through cognition, nor only through the affections. It is crucially a function of the will and well-formed desires, shaped by many different experiences: family upbringing, school, sports, the arts, struggle, reading, dialogue, conflict, reconciliation, relationships, physical challenge, cross-cultural encounters. The character-building initiatives that weave these different strands into one integrated message have the most powerful effect.

Movements in health, education, workplace culture, economic development, and a variety of faith-based initiatives are catching on to this holistic understanding of human nature. You might say the country is seeing a "whole-person revolution" unfurl. Millennials talk about "bringing their whole selves to work." Wharton Business professor Stewart Friedman has said, "Firms that fully embrace the needs and interests of the whole person will win today's competition for the best talent."

But how to move from awareness to implementation? How to shape one's institution, or design a character-building initiative from scratch, to address the whole person?

At Wake Forest University, where educating "the whole person" is the mission, President Nathan Hatch has leavened each academic and administrative department with hires committed to seeing students not just as intellects, but as full moral agents capable of integrating the will, the heart, the head, and the helping hand. It begins with the application for admission, which asks questions like: "Choose an unsung historical figure who deserves the *Hamilton* treatment," or "Hashtags trend worldwide. Give us a hashtag you wish were trending. Why?" These questions invite a form of personal disclosure that is alert to today's world.

Wake Forest now has one of the most sought-after career-service models in the country. Integrating personal development with career development, students study chess and read psychology, philosophy, and history with an eye to discerning their vocation: what they should do and why, who they should be, and what or whom they should serve. They pair up with adult mentors from across the university—faculty, administrators, coaches, custodial staff—to explore the character tests in various career paths: what moral leadership might require in Silicon Valley versus a more traditional corporate job versus medicine versus social work.

Summer camps can also be wonderful examples of whole-person development. Incarnation Camp takes kids out of their normal environment and provides them with an opportunity, away from phones and pressure, to experience the sort of childhood that used to be common. Situated on 700 acres around a mile-long lake in Ivoryton, Connecticut, the campers live in tents, prepare their own meals, go on hiking, canoeing, and bike trips, and conquer their fears. Along with outdoor skills, kids learn to get along with people very unlike themselves.

> Movements in health, education, workplace culture, economic development, and faith-based initiatives are catching on to a holistic understanding of human nature.

The era of metrics and assessment has often given schools an incentive to turn their students into proficient test-takers, but it has not prepared them to be moral leaders. The Great Hearts network in Arizona and Texas believes that the highest goal of education is to become good, intellectually and morally. With a curriculum built upon a classical liberal-arts tradition and extracurriculars that reinforce lessons in character, Great Hearts students practice arts, academics, and athletics with their moral purpose understood as the foundation for their knowledge and skills.

The Gifted Music School in Salt Lake City churns out lots of students who matriculate at Juilliard and Colburn, but its primary goal is to raise well-rounded citizens for the country. "We want to make kids capable of understanding values that are relevant to the survival of our society and our country," says founder Eugene Watanabe. With the discipline required to master technical difficulty, the lessons in public grace and private grit, the honing of musical intuition and deep listening skills, a mentoring relationship with a tutor in the craft, and the unique dialogue with history that the study and performance of classical music invites, Watanabe's view is that the arts impart a constellation of moral traits that can endure for life.

"I truly believe that when children make beautiful music together, in an orchestra, in chamber music, a notion of fundamental respect stays with them," says Watanabe. "Whether they transition into politics, or economics, or business, or law, they carry that fundamental value and respect for others."

6. HEALTHY RELATIONSHIPS
Does the institution put relational health as the foundation for its success? Does the organization foster social trust? Does it have a strong sense of community?

In all my years of working with youth, I've never seen a
program change a life. I've only seen relationships change lives.
~ Bill Milliken, founder of Communities in Schools

Character formation is inherently co-creative. Full human flourishing always comes about through communion, never isolation. Thus we are formed in the context of relationship—relationships with a loving authority figure, historical figures, other exemplars, fictional characters, those you work, befriend, and serve. While proving one's character is itself a volitional act—the individual must choose to submit to be chiseled, must choose to do the right thing, even when it hurts—character is developed in light of relationships past, present, and aspirational future.

You see this affirmed in the three-part pattern described in the introduction. When people describe how their own character has been shaped, they always invoke (1) a relationship with an authority figure, (2) an experience of struggle, and (3) the experience of serving a context greater than self. The first touchstone is key: Love creates life, shapes life, and transforms us. We look to our mothers for cues from the earliest days. Our eyes seek the eyes of others to detect emotion, mood, affirmation, or lack thereof. We naturally learn from those we love and trust, be they mentors, coaches, teachers, or grandparents. Each of these relationships should press us onward and upward, modeling proper behavior and providing a pathway for accountability.

But we live in an era where many relationships have thinned in their power to correct and inspire. We are told to self-isolate in our moral judgments: "You do you" is the colloquial sermon for today's young. Screens are replacing people as purveyors of wisdom and knowledge. Adults—particularly men—struggle to find and sustain friendships, while millennials crow for mentors. Fewer and fewer people grow up under the loving canopy of a whole and attentive family. The daily family dinner has been displaced by sports practices and extracurriculars, long working hours, and the distraction of technology. Social media deludes us into confidence that we understand other people, including their opinions. We have lost patience for an uncontrolled, open encounter, and we fear the messiness of two-way interactions between humans in real time.

More than ever before, we need institutions to model and encourage the healthy relationships fewer and fewer are experiencing.

Community Renewal's consistent testimonies of personal transformation grow out of its intentional relationship-building. The final core value of The Oaks Academy is that "relationships come first in all interactions." The Positivity Project gets elementary- and middle-school kids familiar with their top five character strengths and weaknesses so that these students come to appreciate traits like kindness, curiosity, humility, self-control, and relate to one another more on grounds of character than their classroom smarts, what clothes they're wearing, or how much their parents can or can't afford.

> More than ever before, we need institutions to model and encourage healthy relationships. Positive relationships are key to social and economic improvement.

All Our Kids DC is a 501c3 started by husband-and-wife team David Simpson and Kathy Fletcher. After years of welcoming youth from challenging backgrounds into their home for a hot meal, a bed, and love, Simpson and Fletcher decided to formalize what they were doing so that more adults could mentor and resource their growing brood. This includes helping fund college tuition for the kids who seek it. Now AOK is a thriving, sprawling community where adults serve kids and kids transform adults. Every Thursday evening there's a home-cooked meal. "No cell phones at the table," says Fletcher. "Share yourself." It's become an unconventional family rooted entirely in relationships as the source of material improvement and character change. Some of the adults are now hosting kids in their own homes. Those in college keep in touch with AOK adults across the miles, psychologically strengthened to launch into self-sufficiency, supported by adults who believe in them.

The idea that positive relationships are key to social and economic improvement is gaining ground. More and more of the most effective social programs are speaking in a relational language. Nurse-Family

Partnership helps teenage moms become good parents. Specially trained nurses visit young moms-to-be regularly for two and a half years, starting early in the pregnancy and continuing through the child's second birthday. The nurses counsel the moms about health-promoting behaviors, offering advice on everything from child safety to developmental stages to ways of juggling work and motherhood. Paul Tough, acclaimed author of the bestseller *How Children Succeed*, says that because of NFP, we are seeing reduced incidences of child abuse, arrest, and welfare enrollment. In families where mothers scored especially low on measures of intelligence and mental health, children's academic performance improved.

It sounds soft, and relationships are hard to measure, but if we don't begin there, character loses its moral force.

7. TECH-WISE
Is the institution careful about the latest technological advance, embracing it insofar as it promotes healthy relationships and individual skill, and setting limits when it makes those objectives more difficult?

> *Technology is a useful servant but a dangerous master.*
> **~ Christian Lous Lange**

Technology has become an unavoidable thing in almost all our lives. It is at once a massively promising tool and one that's a force with a logic and power all its own. How do we navigate a world of devices and nonstop distraction, unchaperoned and virtual access to any and everything, and ever-proliferating automation of both basic and complex human tasks?

When it comes to seeking the institutions today that are doing something special in the way of shaping a person's will, mind, heart, and moral compass throughout life, the big elephant in the room is the screen. Our devices present a very real obstacle for all those well-intended efforts to form citizens who are wise, discerning, trustworthy, attentive, courageous, humble, honest, able to disagree without being disagreeable, patient, able to listen deeply, and who love well.

We talk often about what technology is doing to our brains, and there is growing research to deepen our concern. Beyond the brain, technology is also rewiring our habits, our impulses, our rhythms of rest, work, and play, our relationships and our networks of relationships, how we work, and how we engage a common life with others (or don't). In short, the reality of "tech everywhere" touches most if not all of the spheres that shape *and* require character.

The institutions that choose to be discerning about technology are the ones that are likely thinking about character-building the right way. You have to be forceful about this stuff, even radical. You can't just let the forces sweep over you and assume they bring progress. This is again an issue of moral agency, deploying it over and against technology's steamroller, to preserve those spaces in life where deep beauty, goodness, and truth are shared.

All Our Kids DC doesn't allow phones at the dinner table, a rule made to protect a space created to invite those of radically different backgrounds to attend fully to each other. Almost every institution featured in this book—Community Renewal, The Oaks Academy, The

Other Side Academy, The Positivity Project, the historic Boy Scouts—puts thick boundary lines around technology.

Many Montessori Schools, known for their holistic, student-centered educational philosophy, have strict regulations on when technology is allowed and why. Montessori students use computers strictly as a curricular supplement, not as a substitute for books and materials. They view modest tech education as a practical necessity for skills needed in the workplace, such as typing, Excel, search engines, and the like. But beyond that, Montessori schools see technology offering diminishing returns to student development. Their belief is that technology is a useful platform for expressing human capacity that's already been developed. It doesn't help anyone learn the cello, or write a gripping short story, or solve conflict, or discern the proper course in a moral dilemma. If you want an environment to be both formative and creative, technology tends to detract rather than enhance.

> Our devices present a very real obstacle to forming citizens who are wise, discerning, trustworthy, attentive, and able to listen deeply and love well.

Writer and Praxis Partner Andy Crouch articulates a set of questions that every institution intent on character-building should ask before making a decision to embrace the latest technology. He frames them as a series of "technology is in its proper place when..." statements specific to families wrestling with the place of screens in the home, but with a few tweaks. These can apply to any formative institution:

- Technology is in its proper place when it helps us bond with the real people we love. It's out of its proper place when we end up bonding with people at a distance, in an overly controlled and thus contrived and self-serving manner.
- Technology is in its proper place when it starts great conversations. It's out of its proper place when it prevents us from talking with and listening to one another.
- Technology is in its proper place when it helps us take care of the fragile bodies we inhabit. It's out of its proper place when it

promises to help us escape the limits and vulnerabilities of those bodies altogether.

• Technology is in its proper place when it helps us acquire skill and mastery of domains that are the glory of human culture (sports, music, the arts, cooking, writing, accounting, etc.). When we let technology replace the development of skill with passive consumption, something has gone wrong.

• Technology is in its proper place when it helps us cultivate awe for the world we are part of and responsible for stewarding. It's out of its proper place when it keeps us from engaging the wild and wonderful natural world with all our senses.

• Technology is in its proper place only when we use it with intention and care. Technology doesn't stay in its proper place on its own... [rather] it finds its way underfoot all over the house and all over our lives. If we aren't intentional and careful, we'll end up with a quite extraordinary mess.

These statements are deep, for they reveal an orientation toward what we as human beings are ultimately made to do and enjoy. They cause you to ask, "What *is* a home for, ideally? What is a family's purpose, at its heart? How can a school encourage a child to seek the good and discover his or her hidden gifts? What is technology's proper place in a particular company, sports team, artistic endeavor, rehab community, or neighborhood, and how can we keep it there?" The institutions that think hard about these questions, and act on them, are likely attuned to what great character formation requires. Perhaps we should brand such institutions as "Tech-Wise."

8. INTENTIONAL PLURALISM
Does the institution foster opportunities to relate to those unlike yourself? Are members consistently exposed to other worlds, trained in the arts of civility, deep listening, and cross-cultural agility?

Community is not uniformity.... Each one of us is different, one from the other. But all together we are like a symphony, an orchestra; all together we make up a beautiful bouquet of flowers. That means...that we must learn to love difference, to see it as a treasure and not as a threat. Community means the respect and love of difference.... If we let ourselves be attracted to those who flatter us or who are like us, who share our ideas, then we won't grow. Growth will come as we come closer to people who are different from us and as we learn to welcome and listen, even to those who trigger off our pain.
~ Jean Vanier, founder of the L'Arche Communities

Guided encounters with the unexpected can lead to personal transformation, and an awakening to the opportunity for encounter everywhere. When truly working well, an institution that embraces diversity and attends to it properly cultivates lifelong, generative virtues in its members: civility, deep listening, humility, and cross-cultural agility. It produces people who are respectful of those who hold other opinions, who listen before speaking, who seek peace and compromise and not a warrior-like certainty that is dismissive of complexity and the possibility of being wrong. Our fragmented, distrustful world needs such people more than ever.

Washington University law professor John Inazu has a phrase he calls "confident pluralism." He defines it as a temperament that gracefully accepts differences of background, identity, beliefs, and even values, and chooses to reach across the divide to work together toward a common end. Confident pluralists *want* to invest in shared projects with those who hold different views. They seek to build spaces where dialogue and persuasion are a way of life, where diversity is valued as a window on something more universal, and where vulnerability can be aired safely and lead toward deeper understanding.

The task of any character-building institution in the twenty-first century is to impart this civic virtue, for we need human bridges more than ever—people who are third-culture kids, border-stalkers, on the edge of the inside. Intentionally pluralistic institutions help people navigate changing times and deep difference without losing sight of who they are or where they come from. They help people discern the line between timeless truth and temporal expression, and to walk that line with grace and conviction.

The Oaks Academy embraces cultural and socioeconomic difference and attracts 50 percent low-income, 25 percent middle-income, and 25 percent higher-income students, with the racial and ethnic breakdown being 40 percent black, 40 percent white, and 20 percent biracial, Asian, or Hispanic. This human mosaic, while not without its rough edges, shines because The Oaks has a clear telos and an educational philosophy that puts the relationship between all teachers and all students first. Assignments like the capstone eighth grade essay trilogy on truth, beauty, and goodness help students consider how such transcendent ideals apply to each person's unique life experience—aesthetic and moral differences, individual pain, and blessing. Because The Oaks has deliberately cultivated a climate that motivates kids to take hold of their own agency, their differences prepare them to be morally conscious leaders in society. This diversity is neither a divider nor a distraction.

Other programs form confident pluralists by encouraging bridge-building across lines of tribe and worldview. Waldorf schools, for instance, make an international immersion experience mandatory in middle or high school. The Kettering Foundation's initiative Deliberative Dialogue trains college students in the art of civil discourse, hoping to penetrate the current climate of identity politics and withering free speech. Participants hold a substantive discussion around a specific issue by asking questions like, "What are we learning?" "How does this problem affect you and your family?" "What should we do? What would be the consequences?" "Who else do we need to solve the problem?"

9. STRUGGLE & GROWTH
Are there opportunities for growth and tests of character? Does the organization have a process by which such struggles are given meaning and direction?

Character cannot be developed in ease and quiet. Only through experience of trial and suffering can the soul be strengthened, vision cleared, ambition inspired, and success achieved. It is in the most trying times that our real character is shaped and revealed.
~ Helen Keller

While no parent wants his or her child to suffer, every good parent knows that there is no shortcut to cultivating character, and that it's often forged most deeply in and through struggle. Persevering when the going gets tough, overcoming disappointment, accepting the truths that failure can teach, enduring pain, and learning to receive and grant forgiveness for the worst sins strengthen the sinew for wisdom and a generative life. Even if suffering is not automatically ennobling, growth is necessarily yoked to struggle.

When it comes to intentional character-forming initiatives, the best ones incorporate three things: (1) They allow for human struggle if not actively create opportunities for it; (2) They provide a structure for second chances, reflection, and accountability; and (3) They offer a pathway to growth, a chance to prove maturity with greater reservoirs of strength.

Struggle stretches you. It can deepen your empathy for others. It humbles and chastens you. It gives you a more accurate sense of your limitations. Struggle often reveals your true character: Are you selfish when everything you treasure seems threatened? Do you become volatile in times of crisis? Are you able to lead dependents when your world is crumbling? In what do you ultimately put your hope?

Outward Bound and the Boy Scouts have long pushed young people to shoot beyond their physical limits. Whether mountain biking through a dense thicket, bush-whacking with no end in sight, sleeping through dangerous thunderstorms, or climbing a steep rockface, the goal is to surmount daunting challenges. Kids who have been long-time Scouts, or have successfully completed an Outward Bound trip, report greater levels of confidence in themselves and in leading others, a healthy appreciation for the awesome power of the outdoors, a newfound sense for what really matters in life, and a quiet nobility that knows what it is to have overcome their greatest fears, their perceived physical or mental limitations, and to get along with difficult personalities when the circumstances demand teamwork. Struggle is central to both institutions' mission.

Millions of young Americans are shaped by sports, perhaps more than by any other activity. And yet the youth sports culture has grown imbalanced. Youth sports programs often put intense pressure on children, emphasizing winning, and forcing them to perform in order to validate their parents. The Positive Coaching Alliance seeks to transform this culture. The primary formula is better athletes, better people. In the PCA method, coaches have their players (and team as a whole) focus on their effort and personal improvement, rather than simply on the results of the game. They help players recognize that mistakes are an inevitable and important part of the learning process, and that the key to success is the ability to rebound with fresh determination.

10. VULNERABILITY & ACCOUNTABILITY
Is the organization one where members can trust the community and open up with honesty and a desire to be tutored in a better way? Is there a vehicle for grace and second chances? Is there a structure of mutual accountability?

Vulnerability is the birthplace of love, belonging, joy, courage, empathy, and creativity. It is the source of hope, empathy, accountability, and authenticity. If we want greater clarity in our purpose or deeper and more meaningful spiritual lives, vulnerability is the path.
~ Brené Brown

Accountability breeds responsibility.
~ Stephen Covey

Increasingly it seems that the programs considered "interventions"—where dramatic character transformation occurs—have a lot to teach our more gradual character-forming institutions (be they schools, sports teams, or adult learning communities). Some of this may be because the institutions in the business of radical transformation approach their mission with a no-nonsense rigor. Some of it is because those who have seen the ashes of their own choices tend to be the most humble before the hard work that real change demands. We all need a community to show up; the autonomy of life today makes it too tempting to skate. We also all need a community that is as "safe" for vulnerable honesty as it is challenging to our current selves. Where are these character wombs that hold shattered people and then rebirth them? Would we all not be healthier if we were a part of one safe yet rigorous community?

"200% Accountability" lies at the heart of The Other Side Academy's success in moving people from moral kindergarteners to moral heroes. It's peer-to-peer, which is typically the most effective form of accountability, and it's ritualized through "games," the biweekly group confrontation sessions. No ex-offender gets a pass—everyone is scrutinized, and everyone scrutinizes. It works because love is the motivating foundation, each person desiring to help the other improve his or her character and achieve true freedom.

Laity Lodge is an ecumenical retreat center in the Texan hill country born out of the depression of one man—Howard Butt Jr. Over the decades, CEOs, former U.S. presidents, writers, artists, and religious leaders have come to reflect on their vocations, their failures, and the concrete (and less concrete) nature of hope. While associated with an evangelical culture zealous to provide hope and certainty, Laity Lodge makes no such pretensions. Instead of encouraging a perfect facade, the Lodge invites honesty—warts and all. Its compassion and radical hospitality create a space to hold people in times of transition, grief, and searching. In all manner of sin and circumstance, the Lodge graciously allows people to get still and seek higher things. It is a place where people can be safely and truly known, thus opening the door to personal transformation.

Likewise, any addiction-recovery program based on the 12 Steps method (created by the founders of Alcoholics Anonymous) relies on this logic:

1. **Honesty**: Recognizing the addiction and confessing it.
2. **Hope**: Believing that success is possible—not through one's own ability, but through persistence and application.
3. **Faith**: A statement of belief in a power greater than oneself to restore hope and sanity.
4. **Courage**: A scrupulous moral inventory of oneself.
5. **Integrity**: Owning up to one's evaluation of one's assets and shortcomings.
6. **Willingness:** A decision to change one's character and behavior.
7. **Humility**: Acknowledging one's own powerlessness to overcome the addiction alone.
8. **Discipline and Action**: Removing barriers that can block forward sober growth.
9. **Forgiveness:** Committing to making amends with others harmed.
10 **Acceptance:** An ongoing process of owning and admitting one's mistakes and accepting oneself for being imperfect.
11. **Knowledge and Awareness**: Making a conscious effort to do the right thing at every small and large moment, and to seek out one's broader purpose in life.
12. **Service and Gratitude:** Seeking out and being available to help others in need.

What you see here is a tested structure for the routing out of a destructive behavioral pattern. People come to a 12 Steps program desperate, having reached the end of themselves, in need of help, and humble before the realization that they can't free themselves alone. Church small groups have been inspired by the accountability model. Some of the more effective repositories for those experiencing mid-life or even quarter-life crises borrow from this sequence. When a community feels trustworthy, its members are able to be completely honest, which is the only way to get effective help.

11. REFLECTION
Are there built-in processes for reflection, and excavation of one's inner life and public fruits?

We do not learn from experience. We learn by reflecting on experience.
~ John Dewey

Ultimately evil is done not so much by evil people, but by
good people who do not know themselves and who do not probe deeply.
~ Reinhold Niebuhr

We don't live in a highly reflective society. Most of the time we're rushing, seeking efficiency and results. But reflection is vital to our growth. When reflection is guided by a particularly deep listener, or a set of liturgies, it situates a person in his or her broader context—historical setting, present circumstances and relationships, future goals—such that he or she can gain perspective, see blind spots that need to be corrected, and discern the right course of action. Reflection is both a solitary discipline and a communal experience. Other people stir up the stories we tell, the stories we embrace, and the stories we reject. At the end of it all, fruitful reflection yields action, and change.

Open Sky Education manages a growing network of learning environments across the country. With concern for the widening achievement gap, focus among many education reformers has prioritized improving academic scores. Along the way, too many children have lost the opportunity to develop what many have historically considered a key component of education: character.

Open Sky's approach aims to make world-class academics, character formation, and faith-based educational choices accessible and affordable for all. Its Character Formation Project is a licensed program with an easy-to-teach framework, embeddable in everyday conversations, hiring practices, and the dinner table, too.

Early on, Open Sky noticed that the many schools that *were* attempting to weave in a character approach wound up doing behavioral modification instead of genuine virtue development. So it developed three core questions:

1. **Identity:** Who am I? Reputation is who others think that we are. Character is who we really are.

2. **Purpose**: Why am I?
3. **Performance**: How do I live out who and why I am?

Students and teachers spend time throughout the school year reflecting on each of these as they grow, through experience, struggle, triumph, and grace. The beauty is that the questions are transportable: They can be "used" at the dinner table, in a religious context, the locker room, or with a piano teacher. They prompt conversation for both individual and communal understanding and improvement.

Houston Innovators is a vocational incubator for new companies. The year-long program helps budding social entrepreneurs focus on the guiding purpose and principles of their work, with intensive self-examination. Houston Innovators provides a workspace, human capital, mentoring, training, coaching, and networking connections, and each month of gathering together over a two-day retreat involves reading in communion, reflective outpourings both alone and together, and documentation of progress. The hope is that tentative innovators become driven entrepreneurs, anchored in a deep place and moving to "new rhythms from the soul."

> Reflection is both a solitary discipline and a communal experience. Other people stir up the stories we tell. And at the end, fruitful reflection yields action and change.

Students on college campuses today are expressing a deep hunger for wisdom, and finding little to satiate it in their classes or elsewhere. The Veritas Forum helps university communities "ask life's hardest questions." Students, chaplains, and professors plan and organize the events, featuring A-list speakers—such as psychologist Steven Pinker, Pulitzer Prize-winning author Marilynne Robinson, and theologian N. T. Wright—who have thought deeply about how their work integrates with their worldview. Recent topics have included "The Closing of the Modern Mind" with Jonathan Haidt and Tim Keller, "Is There Something More to the Universe?" with Oxford mathematician John Lennox, and "What Do We *Really* Know about Right and Wrong?" with J. Budzisewski.

At this point, over 200 universities in North America and Europe have hosted 2,000 events and counting. Many students report that the Veritas Forum is one of the few, if not only, places on their college campuses where controversial questions of the highest magnitude get a free and open hearing.

The public square more broadly is increasingly void of moral content and curiosity, and there are few models of engagement where people of good will can present and debate topics that are marginalized or deemed too contentious. The Trinity Forum exists to "contribute to the transformation and renewal of society through the transformation and renewal of leaders." Since its founding in 1991, the Trinity Forum has facilitated seminars, discussions, retreats, and lectures for thousands of leaders in North America, Europe, and Asia. These events feature profound reflection and candid conversation about life's most important questions. Speakers including James Davison Hunter, Makoto Fujimura, and Francis Collins focus on topics such as the life and work of Dietrich Bonhoeffer, the complex connection between science and faith, and the dynamic relationship of politics and religion.

The Trinity Forum also produces a broad but focused body of classic and thoughtful writings designed to facilitate conversation and reflection around themes of character, leadership, freedom, civil society, progress, reform, philanthropy, and more.

"People won't automatically imagine something—or have the imagination for something—until they see it," says Trinity Forum president Cherie Harder. "We're giving them something to see."

12. EXEMPLARS

Are there attentive and conscientious authority figures who serve as role models, coaches, and mentors? Does the leader set the character standard for the organization?

> *The heart cannot be taught in a classroom intellectually, to students mechanically taking notes.... Good, wise hearts are obtained through lifetimes of diligent effort to dig deeply within and heal lifetimes of scars....You can't teach it or email it or tweet it. It has to be discovered within the depths of one's own heart when a person is finally ready to go looking for it, and not before.*
>
> *The job of the wise person is to swallow the frustration and just go on setting an example of caring and digging and diligence in their own lives. What a wise person teaches is the smallest part of what they give. The totality of their life, of the way they go about it in the smallest details, is what gets transmitted.*
>
> *Never forget that. The message is the person, perfected over lifetimes of effort that was set in motion by yet another wise person now hidden from the recipient by the dim mists of time. Life is much bigger than we think, cause and effect intertwined in a vast moral structure that keeps pushing us to do better, become better, even when we dwell in the most painful confused darkness.*
>
> **~ Dave Jolly, veterinarian**

Returning to our working definition of character, exemplars are critical. Let's revisit it:

Character is a set of engraved dispositions to serve others and do good. This disposition is carved on multiple fronts and on multiple levels by:

- Strong family attachments that teach what to love and how to love well.
- Regular habits that teach small acts of self-control.
- Teachers and role models who personify excellence and inspire emulation.
- Professors and clergy who demonstrate what it means to be honest, courageous, and compassionate, and how to pursue these things intentionally.
- Mentors and institutions that establish standards for and habits of good conduct.
- Experiences of struggle, positions of responsibility, and the blessings and requirements of enduring commitments. The habits of character

grow best in contexts that are orderly and predictable, with clear, humane feedback mechanisms, and an inspiring ideal in view.

Exemplars are vital to building an intuitive, full understanding of what it means to be a good person and to do good, what it means to lead, what it means to be a contributing citizen, a selfless mother, a dependable neighbor, an honorable athlete. We can read about the virtues, and at the end of the day we all have to face ourselves, but it's moral exemplars that show us *how* to be, through a thousand instances of mannerism, action, personality, and choice.

The sector that understands this most profoundly is education. When you're with children, and you're a good teacher, you know that you're being watched by dozens of impressionable eyes. You're aware that how you behave is going to leave an imprint on still-moldable brains, bodies, and hearts.

But there are also sports, music lessons, the workplace, the family, and even the broader public square. The exemplary individuals in each of these spheres teach us by example, encourage us in conversation, guide, tutor, correct, and inspire. The best ones also instill a sense of responsibility to meet the standard they've set. We emulate those we love; we also hate disappointing them.

Some organizations set up a mentoring structure explicitly. Nurse-Family Partnership's entire model is based on the relationship between a nurse and a first-time mom. New City Kids in Jersey City has instituted a three-layered approach. It hires 150 high-school students to be role models in the after-school program. The younger kids—many of whom lack good role models at home—see themselves in the high-school mentors and strive to assume their roles one day with good behavior. Each high-school student is also assigned an adult mentor to meet with on a regular basis. When big life decisions arise and crises hit, there is a trusted adult to call. The kids attend life-skills classes including money management, résumé crafting, and coaching on the college transition. Students visit companies and speak with employees about the nature of their work and how they got to where they are. New City conducts three performance reviews each year of the students' individual progress, and the high schoolers can apply for leadership positions on staff.

Others have the cross-generational dynamic woven in to the very fabric of the community. Nyack College's educational experience is enriched because grandmothers study alongside 19-year-olds. Ask today's young people whom they admire most, and chances are they'll mention a grandparent. This may be for reasons of distinctive character in the Greatest Generation, but it also could be the interesting nature of authority that one gap in a generational line grants. Whatever the explanation, organizations that foster relationships between old and young are doing something right.

Some organizations go out of their way to train the mentors. The Positive Coaching Alliance equips coaches to devote "teachable moments" to their players' personal improvement and resilience.

While many young people clamor explicitly for mentors today, often the actual investment required seems to keep these same folks at bay. The Internet offers a quick fix for the quotidian questions one would normally ask a peer or authority figure. Technology generally has reduced people's face-to-face engagement to emojis and words on a screen, without the inefficient yet far richer exchange that in-person encounters bring. The individualism that has permeated just about every formative institution in our society has weakened the appreciation for adult chaperones, adult authority, and adult attentiveness. The erosion of friendship—particularly amongst busy adults—has also led people to feeling like they are accountable to no one (and cared about by no one). The organizations that fight all these tendencies are to be encouraged and strengthened.

13. AGENCY & INITIATIVE
Are members of the organization empowered to act, create, initiate? Are they encouraged to be responsible moral agents, not simply passive consumers?

Part of living consists of learning, personally and vicariously, what actions produce what consequences. When we govern ourselves by correct principles, we also govern our consequences. As men "act according to their wills," there are consequences, good and bad. Part of maturing…is to realize this.
~ Neal A. Maxwell

Our culture has done a great job at forming the intellect. It's done a terrible job at forming the will. So just what does equipping the will entail? Who is modeling the necessary conditions for moral agency to be claimed? How do we prepare people to make good judgments in a wide variety of circumstances?

Jeff and Laura Sandefer's Acton Academy has pioneered an education model that empowers kids to teach themselves. Its goal is "to inspire each child and parent to find a calling that will change the world." Acton motivates its students to see life as a Hero's Journey, where someone with curiosity and character can use their innate gifts for good. Each child will:

• Begin a Hero's Journey.
• Learn to be a curious, independent lifelong learner.
• Develop a deep respect for economic, political,
  and religious freedoms.
• Cherish the arts, wonders of the physical world, and the mysteries
  of life on Earth.
• Discover his or her most precious gifts and learn to use them to
  solve difficult problems.

Socratic Discussions and self-paced challenges equip children to be self-directed learners. Hands-on quests in science, entrepreneurship, and the arts prepare children for apprenticeships and real-world challenges. The Hero's Journey, relational covenants, and real-world consequences use difficult decisions to form virtuous habits. As a result, Acton is guiding students who are uniquely self-motivated, primed for leadership, and creative, yet sensitive to the demands of a team.

Both established and emerging leaders increasingly say they cannot function without certain support systems, and without the daily work of deeper leadership development. Yet, leaders do not always have adequate language for what has aided their development and how they have become who they are. Groups like the Woodstock Arrupe Program, Acton MBA, Praxis Labs, Henry Crown Fellows, Gotham Fellows, and the Skoll Foundation offer incubators for leaders to spend time in discernment in a relaxed yet structured setting, and to slowly realize new ideas through a process of deep reading and reflection, dialogue, and some real-world experiments. The goal is to send participants back to their daily lives inspired and equipped with both practical wisdom and a sense of strengthened purpose.

14. JOY
Is there joy in the house? Are hospitality and unconditional welcome a key part of the institution's DNA?

The joy of heaven will begin as soon as we
attain the character of heaven, and do its duties.
~ Theodore Parker

It may sound like Oprah, but the presence of joy is almost always a sign that a community is doing something right. From ancient religious wisdom to contemporary education experts, history locates joy as *the* fruit of a well-ordered life. When you perceive this glow in a community—be it a school, a neighborhood, a synagogue, a salon, a company, a volunteer effort, even a prison—it should be a signal that most if not all of these 16 Questions are being answered with distinction.

Joy is difficult to define, but most of us know it when we see it. It is the fulfillment we get in surrendering ourselves to some noble cause or unconditional love. It is born in contexts where people feel united with those around them, when they find themselves serving a higher ideal, when they are giving themselves to something good, true, and beautiful. Joy is more textured than happiness; it comes through moral struggle, surrender, surprise moments of transcendence. Joy is the crown of a well-lived life. It satisfies the soul.

Long celebrated and cultivated in major religious traditions and non-Western cultural norms, joy is now making a comeback in modern social science, as well as in the work of those studying how human beings learn.

"You know that authentic, transforming learning is happening when you walk into a classroom and you get a palpable sense of joy," says David Steiner, executive director of the Institute for Education Policy at Johns Hopkins School of Education. The Harvard Grant Study, one of the world's longest surveys of adult life, has found that the people who were most satisfied in their relationships at age 50 were the healthiest at age 80. Their ability to withstand the toll of aging was directly related to the joy they had in the context of committed relationships—more important than career success, more important even than taking scrupulous care of their bodies.

At The Other Side Academy in Salt Lake City, people have seen and contributed to life's underbelly. Some have stolen, some have murdered. They've all lied. They've all cheated. But here, in the context of peer-to-peer accountability and people who believe in unfurling their better angels, there is a palpable sense of delight as they learn to respect and trust others—and themselves.

Jean Vanier is a Canadian Catholic philosopher who founded the L'Arche communities that have reached over 8,000 handicapped and disabled people worldwide. L'Arche holds that everyone has needs and gifts, regardless of apparent capacity. Henri Nouwen, who lived at a L'Arche community for the last ten years of his life, experienced a joy there completely counter to the mainstream world's understanding of value. He explained: "When we honestly ask ourselves which person in our lives means the most to us, we often find that it is those who, instead of giving advice, solutions, or cures, have chosen rather to share our pain and touch our wounds with a warm and tender hand."

> Joy is now making a comeback in modern social science, as well as in the work of those studying how human beings learn.

Homeboy Industries in Los Angeles provides training and support to former gang members and other ex-offenders, allowing them to redirect their lives and become contributing members of the community. Each year over 10,000 come through its doors. They are welcomed into a community of mutual kinship, love, and a wide variety of services ranging from tattoo removal to anger management and parenting classes. Full-time employment is offered to more than 200 men and women at a time through an 18-month program that helps them re-identify who they are in their community.

"We choose to infuse hope in kids for whom hope is foreign," Homeboy founder Father Greg Boyle says. "No kid is seeking something in a gang. They are all fleeing something."

There is a transcendent association with true joy. Joy is often found in faith-based institutions, though not exclusively so. It graces people working and living in harmony and self-sacrifice. It is a mischievous function of the last becoming first, and the first becoming last.

15. TRANSFORMATION
Are there consistent testimonies of whole-person change in a positive direction?

Change is the essence of life; be willing to surrender
what you are for what you could become.
~ Reinhold Niebuhr

Ultimately, character formation is about transformation. Sometimes it happens dramatically and overnight; other times it's a more gradual process. Like joy, transformation is a sign of effectiveness, of these 16 Questions answered well.

The kinds of transformations to look for as a character-builder are: From selfish to selfless. From sullen to joyful. From passive to responsible. From insecure to other-centered. From engaged online to engaged offline. From proud to humble. From self-concerned to leading others.

Institutionally, there are often two ways to think about this: intervention programs (The Other Side Academy, a 12 Steps program, Homeboy Industries, a three-day retreat), and long-term character incubators (the family, a school, a neighborhood, an artistic discipline). As a society, we've gotten better at the interventions while letting the permanent structures go.

The Other Side Academy speaks the language of transformation from sunup to sundown. It has a process for achieving dramatic results in each of its wounded and wounding individuals, and banks on it as the hope for each entering resident.

The Positivity Project deals in more gradual transformation. Through its strengths-finding tests, teachers come to realize that the brightest math student needn't be the only student they attend to—that there are other qualities worth encouraging and applauding.

The 12 Steps program boasts dramatic, if gradual, change. Substance addiction is often so deep that it requires constant care and group support. Its common refrain returns again and again to our helplessness and need for grace, for others, for a second chance.

Gap-year programs with a moral bent transform young people from small in scope and mindset to empathetic citizens who can bridge divides, listen to foreign opinions, appreciate the complexities of poverty, and so on.

The National Advanced Academy of Teacher Education offers a two-year program to develop the nation's top-tier educators for improved student and school performance. Through Socratic dialogue and case studies, NAATE attracts experienced teachers who have already been identified as high-performers and immerses them in an intense, residential program that links their daily practice to key theories and principles of education. Teachers gain tools to enhance their classroom practice, and hone leadership skills with peers and other adults outside the classroom. Graduates of the program walk away with a much deeper understanding of, zest for, and commitment to their educational vocation. They describe both the tight-knit peer community and the practice-based inquiry as being transformative to their professional and personal selves.

The key is to ask: Are people being transformed by this experience, these relationships, the embedded norms? Are they going from bad to good, good to great, passive to active, selfish to selfless?

16. GENERATIVITY

When people depart from this formative institution, do they promote a similar culture in other contexts? Has the institution imparted a set of ideals that members want to live up to ever after?

Nothing that is worth doing can be achieved in our lifetime; therefore we must be saved by hope. Nothing which is true or beautiful or good makes complete sense in any immediate context of history; therefore we must be saved by faith. Nothing we do, however virtuous, can be accomplished alone; therefore we must be saved by love. No virtuous act is quite as virtuous from the standpoint of our friend or foe as it is from our standpoint. Therefore we must be saved by the final form of love which is forgiveness.
~ Reinhold Niebuhr

The ultimate sign of an outstanding institution is that those who have passed through it go on to embody and inspire similar values elsewhere. I will call this ripple-effect test "generativity."

Nyack College in New York City is at once energetically Christian and yet urban and ethnically diverse. Most Protestant colleges in the country tend to draw from white evangelical families from the suburbs. Nyack's downtown campus is made up of African Americans, Latinos, Koreans, Vietnamese, Chinese, Africans, and other immigrant students, most of whom hail from storefront churches in the city's outer boroughs.

The first time I visited Nyack, I was struck by a palpable sense of joy, courage, and a radical hospitality. "Where love has a name" was the phrase that kept coming to mind. I asked the faculty what employers testified about Nyack graduates, who typically go on to work in the social sector, from nursing, to serving in homeless shelters, to counseling, to prison work. The faculty answered unanimously: "Employers tell us that our students create mini-Nyacks wherever they go."

This was a powerful statement about institutional impact, and the ability students had gained to go out and foster similar conditions for others, even in places already set in their ways. It suggested that Nyack imparted a particular logic, a way of perceiving reality and relating to others, that students were able to share effectively in other contexts.

Williamson College for the Trades also does this. Students aspire to become "the Williamson Man" throughout their study and apprenticeship, learning values of integrity, self-sacrifice, concern for others, trustworthiness. They graduate and join construction companies, architectural firms, gardening squads, and plumbing units. Employer after employer testifies to the long-term influence of Williamson men—they lead, they model inspiring behavior, and they serve. An identity took root in their formative years, blossomed, and planted new seeds wherever they go. This is how cultures are made.

Psychologist Erik Erikson coined the term "generativity" to describe the stage of maturity in psycho-social development. In contrast to adolescence, when the personality is focused on self more than the needs of others, generativity is the stage at which one can make commitments even to future generations. This goes for institutions as well as individuals.

> Generativity is the stage at which a person can make commitments to future generations, instead of focusing on self.

Case studies on organizations with socially generative practices find that these groups experience low turnover, low levels of internal conflict, high levels of motivation, participation, and trust, a strong sense of belonging, a culture of caring, promotion of personal development and spin-offs, a long-term timescale, and an orientation towards the needs of the surrounding community.

CONCLUSION

Character really is destiny.
When I began this project in the spring of 2016, I didn't know where it would take me, nor, more importantly, the philanthropists I was seeking to serve and equip. The country was embroiled in a bitterly divisive presidential fight, and a crisis of solidarity was cracking up along political, racial, and class lines.

Fast-forward three years and thousands of miles listening to civic leaders, community healers, philanthropists, and moral thinkers, and I began to see "character" as a central thread woven through the searching aches of our time. Everywhere I went, people's ears perked up when they heard that a philanthropic movement to advance character was in the works, and they usually had something to recommend. Americans still care about this mysterious thing called character—deeply—and while they may not always agree on what it is or how to cultivate it, they do agree that if we lose a shared ethos as a society, a uniting set of moral commitments, we will go down like Rome and every other great civilization that rotted first from within and then from without.

The question is: Is it too late? Has our emphasis on self grown beyond intervention? Are we so diverse and polarized on matters of primary principle that restoring a solid moral foundation is a fool's errand?

If the examples in these pages are any signal, I think not. For every coarse lyric and incendiary tweet, for every violent act, public scandal, and disturbing uptick in despairing attitudes and broken homes, there are hundreds of organizations and thousands of citizens working diligently and creatively to serve the common good, to intervene mercifully in fragile lives, and to build up moral strength.

This book tries to bring to life the best of these organizations, and then identifies the conditions that make them successful. I often would think during reporting trips, "Why can't my life be like this? How do I cultivate these conditions in my own home, my office, my neighborhood, every sphere in which I work, relate, create, and contribute? Also, why isn't this everywhere? This level of intentionality, of attention to the other, of hard work without giving up, of radical honesty and relentless striving for the good?" It's striking in a world of social decay and moral numbness when a community refuses the superficial and the cynic, and instead revels in wholesome delight in the good, and in one another. Each of the best site visits felt like a once-in-a-year special occasion, like the organization must have been putting on a show for me, the curious outsider. And yet this is how they behave every day.

Character development is demanding, and there are no shortcuts. At the same time, it is not a matter of trying very, very hard until we finally learn to keep things under control. This was never going to be a book about creating so many more perfect people. This is a book about love, and pain, and those communities that hold both. It's a book about loss, self-sacrifice, and our own poverty of becoming. It's a book about strength shining through weakness, and wrestling and imperfection and stumbling and more.

Mack McCarter from Community Renewal in Shreveport has a saying: "Every door to character-building must be hinged to love and the preciousness of the other." To begin anywhere else is a waste. Ultimately, when it comes to character, we're shaped by the things and people who mean the most to us. In part because they command our affection and respect, but also simply because of our natural inclination to spend more time with them. How to reknit positive relationships into the fabric of society, and the norms and institutions that foster such relationships? How to find our villages, and help others find theirs?

I've tried in this book to help you visualize the conditions for this kind of character-driven village-making, conditions that I have found consistent in those communities that are shimmering with moral coherence and molding admirable people. There was a curious refrain that repeated itself by leaders of the most impressive character-building initiatives, and it went like this: "It's like we know the cure for cancer but are just keeping it a secret. We've known for decades how to help people transform their lives. We just haven't made it accessible to the millions and millions who need it."

From education to addiction recovery, sports to neighborhood revitalization, the institutions doing the most transformative work speak a common language. It is a language of personalism and relationality, hospitality and recognition of the human soul. And these character-builders—whether they self-identify as such or not—are energized and ready to learn from one another, collaborate, and reach as many people as are humble and willing to trust.

Some Explanations

In undertaking a project around character in an age when no one defini-tion rules and there is a dizzying array of entry points to the discussion, I had to make some clear decisions in service of producing achievable les-sons and goals. For every one of the character initiatives featured in this book, there were a couple dozen worthy alternatives but, significantly, hundreds not chosen. Here's why I made the choices that I did, choices that I hope will influence your own thinking and giving.

First, I made a conscious decision to spend more time on an over-arching framework for character-forming *institutions*, less on how to measure or develop individual character traits. Defining terms is important, and proper measurement can be helpful, but it is my experience that spending all one's time isolating the components of something this core to human personality not only leaves out cru-cial elements, but overlooks the very nature of character. This is a holistic enterprise, requiring a deep understanding of the social and moral conditions that allow for healthy attachments to form, that order one's loves, provide opportunities for action, habit-training, and struggle, and that sensitize members to ideals beyond themselves. There's a dearth of sociological and institutional thinking in today's character field, which would go a long way toward helping influ-ential voices within the movement advance beyond word wars and celebrate how character actually gets built. If it's true that character is better caught than taught, formed through practice, not pontification, then we need to learn from what's working, and build from there.

Second, I have not easily answered that common philanthropic ques-tion: Can it scale? As Paul Tough, the author of *Helping Children Succeed*, says, "Scaling up doesn't work as well in social service and education as it does in the tech world." Certainly when we look at our own lives, it becomes clear that who we are stems from the mysterious alchemy of particular relationships, life experiences, narratives, and earned convic-tions. There shouldn't be a McDonald's of character. Rather, the most formative institutions for most people—the thickest ones—tend to be closed systems.

So what does this mean for donors wanting to make an impact? It means that they have to turn their wills and imaginations toward grow-ing these kinds of institutions at a local level. In the 16 Questions, I have offered what I hope is a scalable *logic*, one that can be embodied in dif-ferent ways in different contexts.

Third, and finally, I did not limit my inquiry to organizations that claim to be in the character business. Rather, understanding the question of character in today's America as inextricably linked to the question of community, I widened the scope to find those organizations that improve relationships, that value the social fabric, that may have other ends in view—health, economic empowerment, rehabilitation—but in so doing transform people's behavior and moral sense. Many explicit character-forming efforts seem to approach their mission didactically, as if you can "teach character" the way you might math or history or physics. This is not to dismiss the good work of organizations being intentional, but it *is* to get donors to think more humanely about the rich ecosystem involved in shaping people to be and do good. An ecosystem that our civil society sorely needs to regrow.

So let us step forward with a fresh purpose. If we refuse cynicism and begin where we are, we may be surprised at how life-giving the cultivation of healthy communities and whole people is. Goodness is inherently attractive: A movement built around the people and communities that best embody it should be uniquely unifying, uplifting, generative. After all, at the center of the most beautiful people and institutions we meet is a glad but tremendous obedience to something—to a craft, to a healing cause, to friendship, to God. Such exemplars showcase the moral life as to make others fall in love with it. They invite us freely to "come and see," trusting that upon witnessing the unparalleled joys of exemplary living, we too will be devoted to the lifelong venture of going further up and further in.

INDEX

ABOUT THE PHILANTHROPY ROUNDTABLE

The Philanthropy Roundtable is America's leading network of charitable donors working to strengthen our free society, uphold donor intent, and protect the freedom to give. Our members include individual philanthropists, families, corporations, and private foundations.

Mission
The Philanthropy Roundtable's mission is to foster excellence in philanthropy, to protect philanthropic freedom, to assist donors in achieving their philanthropic intent, and to help donors advance liberty, opportunity, and personal responsibility in America and abroad.

Principles
- Philanthropic freedom is essential to a free society
- A vibrant private sector generates the wealth that makes philanthropy possible
- Voluntary private action offers solutions to many of society's most pressing challenges
- Excellence in philanthropy is measured by results, not by good intentions
- A respect for donor intent is essential to long-term philanthropic success

Services
World-class conferences
The Philanthropy Roundtable connects you with other savvy donors. Held across the nation throughout the year, our meetings assemble grantmakers and experts to develop strategies for excellent local, state, and national giving. You will hear from innovators in K-12 education, economic opportunity, higher education, national security, and other fields. Our Annual Meeting is the Roundtable's flagship event, gathering the nation's most public-spirited and influential philanthropists for debates,

how-to sessions, and discussions on the best ways for private individuals to achieve powerful results through their giving. The Annual Meeting is a stimulating and enjoyable way to meet principled donors seeking the breakthroughs that can solve our nation's greatest challenges.

Breakthrough groups
Our Breakthrough groups—focused program areas—build a critical mass of donors around a topic where dramatic results are within reach. Breakthrough groups become a springboard to help donors achieve lasting effects from their philanthropy. Our specialized staff of experts helps grantmakers invest with care in areas like anti-poverty work, philanthropy for veterans, and family reinforcement. The Roundtable's K-12 education program is our largest and longest-running Breakthrough group. This network helps donors zero in on today's most promising school reforms. We are the industry-leading convener for philanthropists seeking systemic improvements through competition and parental choice, administrative freedom and accountability, student-centered technology, enhanced teaching and school leadership, and high standards and expectations for students of all backgrounds. We foster productive collaboration among donors of varied ideological perspectives who are united by a devotion to educational excellence.

A powerful voice
The Roundtable's public-policy project, the Alliance for Charitable Reform (ACR), works to advance the principles and preserve the rights of private giving. ACR educates legislators and policymakers about the central role of charitable giving in American life and the crucial importance of protecting philanthropic freedom—the ability of individuals and private organizations to determine how and where to direct their charitable assets. Active in Washington, D.C., and in the states, ACR protects charitable giving, defends the diversity of charitable causes, and battles intrusive government regulation. We believe the capacity of private initiative to address national problems must not be burdened with costly or crippling constraints.

Protection of donor interests
The Philanthropy Roundtable is the leading force in American philanthropy to protect donor intent. Generous givers want assurance that their money will be used for the specific charitable aims and purposes they

believe in, not redirected to some other agenda. Unfortunately, donor intent is usually violated in increments, as foundation staff and trustees neglect or misconstrue the founder's values and drift into other purposes. Through education, practical guidance, legislative action, and individual consultation. The Philanthropy Roundtable is active in guarding donor intent. We are happy to advise you on steps you can take to ensure that your mission and goals are protected.

Must-read publications
Philanthropy, the Roundtable's quarterly magazine, is packed with useful and beautifully written real-life stories. It offers practical examples, inspiration, detailed information, history, and clear guidance on the differences between giving that is great and giving that disappoints.

We also publish a series of guidebooks that provide detailed information on the very best ways to be effective in particular aspects of philanthropy. These guidebooks are compact, brisk, and readable. Most focus on one particular area of giving—for instance, how to improve teaching, charter-school expansion, support for veterans, programs that get the poor into jobs, how to invest in public policy, and other topics of interest to grantmakers. Real-life examples, hard numbers, first-hand experiences of other donors, recent history, and policy guidance are presented to inform and inspire thoughtful donors.

The Roundtable's *Almanac of American Philanthropy* is the definitive reference book on private giving in our country. It profiles America's greatest givers (historic and current), describes the 1,000 most consequential philanthropic achievements since our founding, and compiles comprehensive statistics on the field. Our *Almanac* summarizes the major books, key articles, and most potent ideas animating U.S. philanthropy. It includes a 23-page timeline, national poll, legal analysis, and other crucial—and fascinating—finger-tip facts on this vital piece of American culture.

Join the Roundtable!
When working with The Philanthropy Roundtable, members are better equipped to achieve long-lasting success with their charitable giving. Your membership in the Roundtable will make you part of a potent network that understands philanthropy and strengthens our free society. Philanthropy Roundtable members range from Forbes 400 individual givers and the largest American foundations to small family

foundations and donors just beginning their charitable careers. Our members include:

- Individuals and families
- Private foundations
- Community foundations
- Venture philanthropists
- Corporate giving programs
- Large operating foundations and charities that devote more than half of their budget to external grants

Philanthropists who contribute at least $100,000 annually to charitable causes are eligible to become members of the Roundtable and register for most of our programs. Roundtable events provide you with a solicitation-free environment.

For more information on The Philanthropy Roundtable or to learn about our individual program areas, please call (202) 822-8333 or e-mail main@PhilanthropyRoundtable.org.

ABOUT THE AUTHOR

Anne Snyder directs The Philanthropy Roundtable's Character Initiative, a program that seeks to help foundations and business leaders strengthen the "middle ring" of morally formative institutions in the United States. She is also a fellow at the Center for Opportunity Urbanism, a Houston-based think tank that explores how cities can drive opportunity for the bulk of their citizens, and a senior fellow at The Trinity Forum. From 2014 to 2017 Anne worked for Laity Lodge and the H. E. Butt Family Foundation in Texas, and before that, the Ethics and Public Policy Center, *World Affairs Journal,* and the *New York Times.* She has published in *Atlantic Monthly,* the *Washington Post, City Journal,* and elsewhere, and is a contributing editor to *Comment Magazine* and a trustee at the Center for Public Justice. Anne spent the formative years of her childhood overseas before earning a bachelor's degree from Wheaton College (IL) and a master's degree from Georgetown University. She currently lives in Washington, D.C.